D1125226

The
PROMISE
of
CHRISTMAS

25 Reflections for Advent

JOHN GRECO

Our Daily Bread
Publishing™

Previously published as *Manger King: Meditations on Christmas and the Gospel of Hope* (Discovery House, 2015).

Requests for permission to quote from this book should be directed to: Permissions Department, Our Daily Bread Publishing, PO Box 3566, Grand Rapids, MI 49501, or contact us by email at permissionsdept@odb.org.

Library of Congress Cataloging-in-Publication Data

Names: Greco, John, author.
Title: The promise of Christmas : 25 reflections for Advent / John Greco.
Description: Grand Rapids, MI : Our Daily Bread Publishing, [2021] |
  Summary: "John Greco presents the historicity and beauty of Christ's
  birth to help you celebrate the greatest miracle of all"-- Provided by
  publisher.
Identifiers: LCCN 2021027360 | ISBN 9781640701168 (paperback)
Subjects: LCSH: Christmas--Meditations. | advent--Meditations. | BISAC:
  RELIGION / Holidays / Christmas & Advent
Classification: LCC BV45 .G718 2021 | DDC 242/.335--dc23
LC record available at https://lccn.loc.gov/2021027360

Interior design by Michael J. Williams

For Jonah
I love you, and I'm proud of you—and I still pray
your life will be full of God-with-us moments.

CONTENTS

PREFACE

"Can we do Christmas again tomorrow, Daddy?" My three-year-old son, Jude, posed that question in the second week of January. Laurin and I had begun to take down the Christmas decorations, and Jude was noticeably not on board with our decision.

Of course, kids love Christmas. What's not to love about presents, candy, and an evergreen in the living room? But I think Jude is onto something. Maybe we should celebrate Christmas tomorrow, and the next day, and the day after that.

Maybe we should celebrate the coming of our King throughout the year. Maybe we should sing songs about angels and shepherds and wise men in the spring and on into the summer. Maybe we should take time out each day to reflect upon the thrill of hope that is the Savior in a manger.

What you're holding in your hands is a Christmas book, and you're probably reading these words at Christmastime. But my prayer is that the short chapters to follow would not become mere decorations for your Advent season. The story of Jesus's birth is not only for Christmastime; it's also meant to shape your life the whole year through.

If you open up your Bible to Matthew or Luke to read about the birth of Jesus, you might notice that there are lots and lots of pages to the left and lots and lots of pages (but not quite as many) to the right. That's because Jesus came neither at the beginning of the story God is telling nor at the end. Christmas is right there in the middle, the turning point. It's the fulfillment of many Old Testament promises, but it's also the start of the new thing God is doing in this world.

So, as you read this little book, I hope you will find yourself caught up in the story of redemption, a true tale that began in the book of Genesis and continues to this day. You're invited to be a part of it, and if you accept God's invitation, you just might find it feels a little bit more like Christmas every day of the year.

ACKNOWLEDGMENTS

I have the world's greatest collaborator, editor, proofreader, coach, and publicist—my bride, Laurin. Though she is officially none of those things on paper, she reads every word I write, and I value her opinion more than any other person's. Thank you, Laurin, for putting up with Christmas talk all year long, and for the cheerleading, gracious feedback, and numerous hours you've let me stare blankly at my laptop screen when I probably should have been doing yard work. I love you.

Thanks also to the team at Our Daily Bread Publishing, who helped bring this book to life the first time around: Andy Rogers, Miranda Gardner, and Dave Branon. With this second edition, I add to that list Dawn Anderson. It is a joy to work with kindred spirits who love words and who cherish the Word of God.

Bits of Christmas Candy

Oh, taste and see that the LORD is good!

—Psalm 34:8

One Christmas many years ago, my sister, Kerry, and I attempted a gingerbread house. Neither of us had ever made one before, and we assumed it would be an easy and fun project to get us in the Christmas mood. After it was too late, we discovered that constructing a house of gingerbread and candy was only slightly less complicated and labor intensive than assembling a real house—and we found out that we were about as qualified to work with sweets and cookies as we were to build with concrete and lumber.

In the end, our gingerbread house was more of a gingerbread hovel—the kind of place gingerbread zoning boards would condemn and even the most impoverished gingerbread citizens would look down upon. It was quite sad. But there is something wonderful about even the most poorly built gingerbread house: It's still made of cookies and candy. Our project may have been a failure, but the pieces were delicious. When it comes to gingerbread houses, the parts can be greater than the whole.

A good story works this way too. A master storyteller is able to weave elements and characters together to engage his or her audience. The completed narrative is itself beautiful and rich, but each detail has a way of giving even more to the reader. Because of this depth, the best stories can be enjoyed on multiple levels. The whole meal can be consumed quickly with all the ingredients being tasted together, or the elements can be savored slowly and individually to reveal nuances that might be missed when mixed with the other flavors. My favorite stories are those in which the details—the ingredients—can, at times, deliver something new.

When we come to the Christmas story in the Bible, the scenes are familiar—so familiar that many of us can no longer see the elements that make it such a great story. It's like a gingerbread house that we've all forgotten is made of candy. We enjoy it on one level—that of a beautiful and meaningful account of the Savior's birth—but we miss it on all the others. There is more to be enjoyed in the story of the first Christmas if we'll stop, break off a piece, and chew on it for a while. The readings on the pages that follow are an attempt to help us do just that.

> How sweet are your words to my taste,
> sweeter than honey to my mouth!
>
> Psalm 119:103

1

More Than a Manger

LUKE 2:8–14

"And this will be a sign for you: you will find a baby wrapped in swaddling cloths and lying in a manger."

—Luke 2:12

At the center of every nativity scene is a manger: full of straw, surrounded by animals, and cradling the newborn baby Jesus. Mary and Joseph look on in adoration. Around them and above them is the frame of a stable—modest but secure. From one side, shepherds arrive with crooks in hand, ready to worship the newborn King. And from the other, as if on cue, come wise men bearing gifts of gold, frankincense, and myrrh. Up in the sky, if the nativity is to be complete, is the Christmas star, which illuminates the stable and sets it apart from the otherwise dark and unwelcoming world.

I remember a ceramic nativity scene my mom would place on a table in our living room every year. As a kid, I wanted to move the wise men across the room somewhere, recalling that Matthew says they arrived when Joseph, Mary, and Jesus were living in a house, which, I reasoned, must have been quite some time after the birth of Jesus (2:11). The star wouldn't yet be above the stable then, since it moved along before the magi (2:9). And I had heard at church that the stable was probably a cave, since barns as we think of them today were rare in ancient Judea. I may have been an odd child, but the details of the story were important to me. Jesus is real, so we ought to get His birthday right, I concluded.

Around the same time I began to critique my mother's crèche, I had begun to memorize Bible verses at school, the first being 2 Timothy 3:16: "All Scripture is God-breathed and is useful for teaching, rebuking, correcting and training in righteousness" (NIV). If God breathed out every word of Scripture, then every word is important. We're missing out if we gloss over certain points or ignore how God himself tells the story. No matter how comfortable and familiar our nativity scenes may be, we're only cheating ourselves if we hold on to tradition at the cost of truth.

Take, for example, the mention of the manger (Luke 2:7, 12, 16). It's a word we hardly ever use outside of a Christmas context. It is so often equated with Jesus's birth that we lose sight of its more basic meaning. A manger is a feeding trough for farm animals; what is placed there becomes food for sheep and oxen.

On the first Christmas night, an angel announced to shepherds in a nearby field, "For unto you is born this day in the city of David a Savior, who is Christ the Lord. And this will be a sign for you: you will find a baby wrapped in swaddling cloths and lying in a manger" (Luke 2:11–12). The manger is part of the sign that the baby Jesus would be Savior, Christ, and Lord. But is the sign merely the peculiarity of finding a baby lying in a feeding trough? Or does the manger point to something more—perhaps to the very manner in which Jesus would save His people?

The sign of the manger is similar to the sign-acts of the Old Testament prophets. Like Isaiah walking naked for three years to illustrate the disgrace about to come upon the Egyptians and Cushites (Isaiah 20) or Ezekiel packing his luggage for the exile (Ezekiel 12:1–7), the newborn King is placed in a manger as a picture of what is to come. The manger is an indication of how

Jesus's life will go. His body will be broken and become life-giving food for sheep that hunger. "And [Jesus] took bread, and when he had given thanks, he broke it and gave it them, saying, 'This is my body, which is given for you. Do this in remembrance of me'" (Luke 22:19).

In Bethlehem, which means "house of bread" in Hebrew, the Bread of Life is born. About thirty-three years later and a few miles to the north in Jerusalem, the Bread would be broken for the many. Tucked into the middle of the nativity scene is more than a humble, makeshift cradle. The manger is a flaming arrow pointing to the cross. This child who has been born the Savior of the world will pay for that salvation at a great cost, His own life.

The King-of-Kings-come-to-earth should have, by all rights, been born in a palace and placed in the most luxuriously appointed cradle imaginable. But that is not how God wrote His story. The manger is an icon of the incarnation, a picture of the Son of God, who "emptied himself, by taking the form of a servant, being born in the likeness of men" (Philippians 2:7). As we know from the rest of Jesus's story, the humility of Christ goes far beyond the taking up of flesh and bones: "he humbled himself by becoming obedient to the point of death, even death on a cross" (Philippians 2:8). And so, in the manger, even before He could lift His head, the infant Son of God set His face toward Jerusalem. Despite the radiant light of angels breaking through the night sky above the nearby countryside, the familiar nativity scene sits in the shadow of the cross.

2

The Christmas Story You've Never Heard

LUKE 2:1–7

And she gave birth to her firstborn son and wrapped him in swaddling cloths and laid him in a manger, because there was no place for them in the inn.

—Luke 2:7

Noah, the only citizen of earth considered righteous in his day (Genesis 7:1), succumbs to drunkenness following God's miraculous rescue of his family. Job, a servant blessed by God as blameless (Job 1:8), questions his Maker's right to do as He pleases. And David, called a man after God's own heart (1 Samuel 13:14), commits adultery and plots murder. By contrast, the consistent portrait of Jesus's mother, Mary, is that of a faithful woman who trusts in the Lord. In a Bible full of heroes gone wrong, Mary stands out as a woman of virtue. Through her, God accomplishes His eternal purposes—without any evidence of stumbling or rebellion on her part.

Beyond what the gospel writers tell us about Mary, her depiction in popular retellings of the Christmas story usually leans in one of two directions. Either Mary becomes a near-angelic creature who gives birth without producing as much as a drop of sweat, or she becomes a tenacious pioneer woman with an indomitable spirit, fearlessly delivering the Christ child in the worst of circumstances, against the elements and against all odds.

Most people today would consider the stylized Mary with nary a hair out of place to be romanticized fiction meant for Renaissance paintings and Christmas cards; the second version is more appealing to modern ears. It's gritty, and therefore it seems more likely, more realistic. It's riveting to think of Mary, full of pluck and determination, falling to her knees on the streets of Bethlehem but refusing to give in to the wind and the cold, or to the hard luck that awaited her in such an unwelcoming town.

But what if both scenes are a bit off? What if both say more about us than they do about the mother God chose for His Son? The first scene I described—the Christmas card scene—makes Mary seem otherworldly. No one looks that good after having just given birth. But the second scene—the bloody, sweaty stable scene—also has little basis in reality, given what the biblical text tells us about Jesus's birth. The truth, I believe, lies somewhere in the middle, and it hinges largely on one word.

In Luke 2:7 we read, "And she gave birth to her firstborn son and wrapped him in swaddling cloths and laid him in a manger, because there was no place for them in the inn." At the risk of robbing small children of a meaty part in the church nativity play, I'd like to suggest that there was no innkeeper in the Christmas story at all. The Greek word *katalyma*, here translated "inn," is probably best understood as "guest room."

We know the word Luke likes to use for "inn." He uses it later when telling the story of the good Samaritan (10:25–37), and the word he uses is *pandocheion*, not *katalyma*. When *katalyma* does show up later in Luke's gospel, it's used with reference to the upper room (or "guest room") inside the house where Jesus and His disciples share their last Passover meal on the night Jesus is betrayed (22:11).

So how does properly defining this one word change the Christmas story? Joseph and Mary were not strangers in a strange city. Most likely, they were welcomed guests in the home of one of Joseph's relatives. After all, Bethlehem was his family's hometown. But because so many people had traveled to register for the census, his relative's guest room was full. So Mary gave birth in the room below, in the area reserved for animals to sleep on cold nights, which was likely the most comfortable spot in the house—given all the extra company. There's no indication that Mary went into labor on the night she and Joseph arrived in Bethlehem; Luke simply tells us she gave birth "while they were there" (2:6). No rejection by the townspeople, no frantic search for a place to give birth. Mary's labor and delivery were likely very similar to the experiences of other women in the first century.

The Christmas story is not the harrowing tale of a virgin mother who defiantly threw aside larger-than-life obstacles to deliver a child in a hostile world. Mary was faithful, obedient, and willing to serve God through extraordinary circumstances. And she was likely scared, as any new mother would be. But God provided for His divinely appointed vessel. Joseph was a righteous man who took great care for Mary's physical needs, even securing relatively comfy accommodations for her to give birth. And I have no doubt that the God to whom she sang praises provided for her spiritual needs, reassuring her when doubts pressed in.

The special details of Jesus's birth bring Him glory—the angels and the shepherds, the wise men and the star. Poor and rich, Jew and Gentile alike—all have reason to worship. And Mary's obedience brings Jesus glory too. But the Christmas story is not mainly about her—it's about her Son, God's Son.

Mary was the first person to meet Jesus in this world, and her life serves as a worthy example for all who come after her. Though we may be tempted to believe that, like the rugged, never-say-die Mary of our imaginations, we must bite our bottom lips in fury and make a way for God in this world, such is not our role in the story. As with Mary, it takes a miracle for God to include us in the story at all. Our job is simply to embrace the miracle, listen for God's voice, and obey.

How Two Guys Named Joseph Rescued the World

MATTHEW 1:18–25

> When Joseph woke from sleep, he did as the angel of the Lord commanded him: he took his wife, but knew her not until she had given birth to a son. And he called his name Jesus.
>
> —Matthew 1:24–25

One of my favorite lines from all of literature is the first one in C. S. Lewis's *The Voyage of the Dawn Treader*: "There was a boy called Eustace Clarence Scrubb, and he almost deserved it." That sentence makes me smile every time I read it. There's something delicious about a name that perfectly describes a person's character or profession, especially when it happens in real life. For example, I once had a coworker who was a strict vegetarian; her name is Josie Rabbitt. And not too far from the first house my wife and I called home is the dental office of Dr. Payne. Sometimes a name just fits a person. This was the case with Joseph, Mary's husband and Jesus's stepfather.

According to Matthew's gospel, Joseph's full name is *Joseph, son of Jacob* (1:16), and the similarities between his story and the story of another biblical Joseph, son of Jacob, are undeniable. Back in Genesis, the first Joseph is a dreamer. He has dreams about what God will do through him in the future (37:5–11). The Joseph of the Christmas story receives dreams from God as well (Matthew 1:20–23; 2:12, 19–20). And just as the first Joseph resists temptation and remains chaste with Potiphar's wife (Genesis 39:10), so the second resists temptation and remains pure with Mary, his pregnant wife, until she gives birth to Jesus (Matthew 1:25). Finally, the patriarch Joseph takes the holy family of God—his father Jacob's household—down to Egypt to save them from coming disaster (Genesis 45–46). In the book of Matthew, the other Joseph does the same for another holy family, taking Mary and the child Jesus down to Egypt (2:14–15).

At the end of the book of Genesis, the first Joseph looks back on his life and sees why God had allowed him such a crooked and sometimes painful path: "to bring it about that many people should be kept alive" (50:20). But at the beginning of the gospel of Matthew, the second Joseph looks ahead and can see—even if through a glass dimly—why God was asking such a strange, difficult thing of him. The angel had told him, "You shall call his name Jesus, for he will save his people from their sins" (1:21). When we consider the lives of both men, a common theme emerges: Both Josephs submit themselves to the Lord, despite the cost, for the good of other people and for the glory of God.

In the nativity story, Joseph discovers that his beloved Mary is pregnant. A woman caught in adultery could be stoned to death according to the law of Moses (Deuteronomy 22:23–24). But Joseph has it in his heart to treat Mary mercifully. Since they are betrothed, he decides to divorce her privately so she won't be put to shame. It's another option available to him (Deuteronomy 24:1). Even though he believes Mary has betrayed him, Joseph's will is bent toward kindness. The inclination of his heart is apparent. But when a messenger from God appears to him in a dream, he puts his own plans—his plans to divorce Mary—aside. Like his Old

Testament namesake, who endured injustice and imprisonment without exacting revenge, Joseph shows himself to be a man strong enough to trust the Lord, even when doing so might prove costly. He believes God's messenger and responds with obedience—the kind of obedience that sees past the letter of the law and into the heart of God.

Joseph seems too good to be true—a man who obeys the Lord without question and thinks of others before himself. But his character was carved out over time. What we see in the birth accounts in Matthew and Luke is the fruit of seeds planted long before his angel-dreams began or he found out Mary was expecting a child.

What's also striking to me is that Matthew records nothing Joseph said. In fact, not a single word from Joseph is mentioned in all of Scripture. Everything we know about Joseph comes as a result of what he does, not what he says. Joseph's actions point to his heart, and his heart is kindled with love for God. Is it any wonder this is the man God chose to be an earthly father for His Son?

4

The Christmas Present under Jesus's Family Tree

MATTHEW 1:1–17; LUKE 3:23–38

And Jacob the father of Joseph the husband of Mary, of whom Jesus was born, who is called Christ.

—Matthew 1:16

Matthew begins his account of Jesus's life and ministry with a genealogy, which to modern eyes is like starting an action movie by rolling the credits. But genealogies served an important purpose in the ancient world. Being able to find your branch of the family tree could settle land disputes, inheritance issues, and bragging rights. In the case of Jesus, it is important for Matthew to show his readers that He is both a descendant of David and the chosen seed of Abraham (1:1). Otherwise, Jesus cannot be the long-awaited King of Israel.

Much ink has been spilled justifying the importance of the first seventeen verses of Matthew. Many commentators point out the three sets of fourteen generations in the genealogy (1:17), which not only explains the selective nature of Matthew's list but also connects

Jesus with David, since the numerical value of David's name in the Hebrew language is fourteen. Still other scholars point to the women who are included in Jesus's family line—Tamar, Rahab, Ruth, Bathsheba (simply called "the wife of Uriah" in 1:6), and Mary—a feature the other genealogies in Scripture don't contain. But I believe there's something more incredible about the genealogy that Matthew provides in his gospel, for it contains within its names a foretaste of the miracle of salvation—the seemingly impossible intersection of God's justice and God's mercy.

In order for Jesus to be the Messiah, He has to be a son of Abraham, for God had promised the patriarch, "In you all the families of the earth shall be blessed" (Genesis 12:3; compare Galatians 3:8). And He has to be a biological descendant of David; God was very specific in His promise to the king: "I will raise up your offspring after you, *who shall come from your body.* . . . I will establish the throne of his kingdom forever" (2 Samuel 7:12–13; emphasis added). Finally, the Christ would need to come from the line of David's son Solomon: "For his name shall be Solomon. . . . He shall build a house for my name. He shall be my son, and I will be his father, and I will establish his royal throne in Israel forever" (1 Chronicles 22:9–10).

But there's a big problem with Solomon's royal line: God cut it off—*permanently.* Jeremiah 22:30 records a curse pronounced against King Jechoniah (also called Coniah and Jehoiachin), one of Solomon's direct descendants: "Write this man down as childless, a man who shall not succeed in his days, for *none of his offspring shall succeed in sitting on the throne of David and ruling again in Judah*" (emphasis added). Although he was king for just over three months (2 Kings 24:8), he was the biological end of a long line of kings in Judah, most of whom were wicked. Like his fathers before him, "he did what was evil in the sight of the LORD" (2 Kings 24:9), so God decreed that none of his children or his children's children—for the rest of time—would ever sit on David's throne.

There were Jewish men in the first century who could trace their lineage back to David. Some, including Joseph, could even trace their ancestral path back up through the royal line of Solomon, but there were none who could do so without also tracing their ancestry back through Jechoniah. To do that would require a miracle.

Jesus is Mary's son biologically, and that makes Him a descendant of Abraham and of David. Luke catalogs Mary's ancestry all the way back to Adam through David's son Nathan (3:23–38), though she herself is not named, in keeping with the standard Jewish practices of the time regarding genealogies. And because Jesus was the firstborn Son adopted by Joseph, He was the legal heir to Solomon's royal line but not subject to Jechoniah's curse, since He isn't Jechoniah's biological descendant, one of his "offspring" (Jeremiah 22:30). Also, because Jesus was born to a virgin and God was His Father, no earthly family could claim Jesus as their own and negate His claim to the throne of the kingdom. Through Jesus, God was able to fulfill His promise to "raise up for David a righteous Branch" (Jeremiah 23:5), despite the end of Solomon's royal line. God was able to remain just, punishing the sin of Judah's kings, all the while keeping His good promises to Abraham, David, and Solomon.

This is what we see in the cross of Jesus as well, which "was to show [God's] righteousness at the present time, so that he might be just and the justifier of the one who has faith in Jesus" (Romans 3:26). We needed a substitute—someone, like Adam, to represent the human race. But no one was able to live a perfect life and offer a perfect sacrifice on our behalf; all of us are infected with the disease of sin. So God, in His mercy, became one of us to do what we could not do on our own. At Calvary, He upheld the laws of justice while showing radical mercy to His creatures, and He overcame Satan's accusations by showing that even our own disobedience cannot thwart God's goodness.

The virgin birth matters. God's choice of Joseph and Mary matters. Long before Jesus was nailed to a tree, His family tree pointed to God's holy design—to the intersection of justice and grace in the promises of God.

5

Shepherds Who Leave Their Flocks

LUKE 2:15–20

And in the same region there were shepherds out in the field, keeping watch over their flock by night.

—Luke 2:8

One year at Christmastime, my wife, Laurin, and I planned to surprise our extended family with the news that Laurin was pregnant with our first child. We bought a bunch of balloons, including an extra-large one in the shape of a rattle with "BABY" printed across it. We had the balloons filled with helium, and then we sealed them inside the biggest box Home Depot sells. We wrapped up the package and placed it under the tree at my sister's house, where we all gathered for Christmas Eve. After dinner had ended and all the other presents were opened, I called my nieces and nephews together and told them there was one more gift to unwrap. With a couple of swipes at the package from some of the older kids, the balloons burst out of the box and hit the ceiling, and so did the room. Our family was overjoyed to hear our news—almost as excited as we were to share it.

Imagine the joy that erupted in heaven the night Jesus was born, the night God's plan of redemption put flesh on and came into our world. It seems the joy was so great that even heaven could not contain it; it came bursting through the night sky outside of Bethlehem as a host of angels praised God and announced to unsuspecting shepherds that the Messiah had been born.

Shepherds hold an esteemed place in Scripture. God is called a shepherd (Genesis 48:15; Psalm 23:1), and many biblical heroes were shepherds, including Jacob, Moses, and King David. Jesus even described himself as "the good shepherd" (John 10:11, 14). But outside of the Bible's pages, shepherds led less-than-glamorous lives in the ancient world. Out on the fringe of society, shepherds walked through life with a staff in one hand and little to hold in the other. Because of their work, they were often ceremonially unclean and not permitted in the temple courts. And in many circles, self-respecting Jews considered shepherds to be dishonest, transient, and unsavory characters. As a result, shepherds were frequently treated as outcasts.

Yet God identified with shepherds. They were the first "family" to hear the news of Jesus's birth, the first to come worship the baby King. God's choice of shepherds fits with the overall theme of the first Christmas. Humble surroundings, unlikely parents, and a life begun in obscurity—all these speak loudly that Jesus would be a King who is not at home with the order of this world. And so too does His welcoming court of shepherds, who likely smelled of sweat and sheep and soil. Jesus was bringing a kingdom where social norms would be turned upside down. As Mary had proclaimed months earlier, "[God] has brought down the mighty from their thrones and exalted those of humble estate" (Luke 1:52). These shepherds were among the first to be exalted.

But these sheepherders serve as more than representatives of the poor and lowly in society. It's likely, given their location outside of Bethlehem, that these were no ordinary shepherds. These men may have been tending the sheep used in the temple sacrifices in Jerusalem. If this was the case, the shepherds' short journey from the fields into town to find the newborn Messiah was a move that would mark the turning of the ages. By leaving their flocks to seek out the Savior, the shepherds were symbolically leaving behind what God had done in the past in pursuit of what God would now do through Jesus. They were, in essence, trading in old wineskins for new (see Matthew 9:17). That Christmas night, when the shepherds received the announcement that the Christ had been born, they received word that the old order had passed away. Something new had come.

The temple system, with its blood and its blades and its burning, showed in graphic detail the costliness of sin and the need for a substitute to pay its price on our behalf. But the cover provided by the animal sacrifices didn't last long. There was always the need for another sacrifice, for another lamb to be slaughtered. The sacrificial system was powerless to provide what we really needed—new hearts, divine forgiveness, and someone to satisfy the wrath of God. Jesus's sacrifice on the cross was a perfect one, forever securing access to the Father for His children.

Whether or not they realized it fully, the shepherds left "the ninety-nine" in search of the one Lamb whose sacrifice would provide everything they needed. "But when Christ had offered for all time a single sacrifice for sins, he sat down at the right hand of God, waiting from that time until his enemies should be made a footstool for his feet. For by a single offering he has perfected for all time those who are being sanctified" (Hebrews 10:12–14).

6

The Only Guests
Who Brought Christmas Gifts

MATTHEW 2:1–12

When they saw the star, they rejoiced exceedingly with great joy.

—Matthew 2:10

It has all the elements of a scene from a modern comedy built on awkward moments. King Herod smiles as he greets dignitaries from the east, along with their entourage of lesser officials, soldiers, and servants. It was a caravan of importance that had just paraded into Jerusalem and petitioned an audience with the king. I imagine Herod thought himself worthy of this dignity, believing he was a man like Solomon, the wisest of his age. It was said of him, "And people of all nations came to hear the wisdom of Solomon, and from all the kings of the earth, who had heard of his wisdom" (1 Kings 4:34). Now, it seems, Herod is receiving the honor of such a visit.

Then one of the state officials—one of the wise men—speaks up, "Where is he who has been born king of the Jews?" (Matthew 2:2). And just like that, the oxygen in the room is replaced with uncomfortable silence. Herod the Great is the builder of cities and the restorer of God's temple, but the magi aren't there to honor him, or even to see him. They have come to Judea with gifts, to recognize—and to worship—another King.

Speaking through the prophet Isaiah, God had declared to Israel, "I will make you as a light for the nations, that my salvation may reach to the end of the earth" (Isaiah 49:6). Solomon's reign had been such a light, attracting the wise and exalted from remote corners of the known world. But Solomon's reign ended, other kings came and went, there was captivity and exile, and all the while Israel's light dimmed.

With the coming of Jesus, Israel's light would shine brightly again as the early church would share the good news of salvation with those outside the Holy Land. The apostle Paul even alludes to Isaiah's prophecy to explain his preaching to the Gentiles (Acts 13:47). But the magi in Matthew's gospel don't wait for an apostle or an evangelist to come to them; they come seeking the light on their own.

They had followed a literal light in the sky to Judea, a mysterious star that had appeared two years earlier and had shown the way to the long-awaited Messiah (see Matthew 2:16). But there are a lot of stars in the sky, a lot of lights one might follow. It seems a strange thing to pick one and start walking. Apparently, the magi had been waiting for such a sign in the sky; they were waiting for a King to be born.

Centuries earlier, there was another wise man—a man named Daniel, who was a leader among the magi in Babylon (see Daniel 2:48). But Daniel was no ordinary wise man; he was a servant of the true God. One of the young men exiled to Babylon from Judea, Daniel faithfully served God while ministering before the kings of Babylon and, later, the kings of Persia. Like the magi in Matthew's gospel, Daniel also waited for a King and a "kingdom that shall never be destroyed" (2:44). He had studied God's Word and knew God's promises (9:2), and he even received angelic answers related to the timing of those promises (9:20–27). However, Daniel himself did not live to see all of God's promises fulfilled. Instead, it seems he left a legacy in Babylon: the Scripture that he loved so dearly and his own writings.

More than five centuries later, Daniel's positional descendants—the wise men of the first century—see that the time has come for God to fulfill His promise of a King. Maybe they gleaned God's prophetic timeline from Daniel's own words, or perhaps they received a divine dream similar to the one they would receive after visiting the Christ child (Matthew 2:12). Either way, the magi know to look for a star in the heavens to mark the coming of the Savior.

Having been trained in ancient astrology—part of the job description for magi—the wise men believe that significant events on earth are sometimes signaled in the night sky. Long before Jesus was placed in a manger and long before Daniel walked the halls of power in Babylon, God had left a clue about the coming King and this unique star on the lips of Balaam, an enemy who prophesied blessings over God's people even while hoping to bring harm to the nation. He said, "I see him, but not now; I behold him, but not near: a star shall come out of Jacob, and a scepter shall rise out of Israel" (Numbers 24:17).

When Jesus is born in Bethlehem, He is born King of the Jews, even while Herod, however illegitimately, holds the scepter in Judea. But Jesus is not only born King of the Jews; He is also born the King of Kings, so it's appropriate that people from other nations, like the wise men, come to honor and worship Him. Their arrival isn't a lucky coincidence or a random occurrence. Though the visit of the wise men was unexpected for Herod—and for Mary and Joseph—it was planned long, long before. When a strange star first appeared above the horizon, their visit was planned. When a slave named Daniel was promoted to prominence in Babylon, their visit was planned. And in the days when God's people camped in the desert and a pagan seer was hired to curse Israel but instead spoke words of blessing, their visit was planned.

No one knows who the wise men were or exactly where they were from. No one knows for sure whether they were influenced by Daniel's writings or by Balaam's prophecy. And no one can say with certainty what made these men follow that particular star in the sky. But we know this: God directed the steps of the magi.

Every follower of Jesus has a unique story. Like proverbial snowflakes in winter, no two are exactly alike. But no matter how long and winding our paths, each of us had a visit that was divinely appointed long ago. Our great God brought Jesus Christ to us, but He has also been working behind the scenes, in the good and the bad and the seemingly random, to direct our steps toward Him.

7

The Unexpected Good News of Christmas

LUKE 2:25–35

"Behold, this child is appointed for the fall and rising of many in Israel, and for a sign that is opposed (and a sword will pierce through your own soul also), so that thoughts from many hearts may be revealed."

—Luke 2:34–35

It's one of the only times we see Linus Van Pelt voluntarily set aside his famous blue blanket during a Peanuts television special. Reciting the King James Version of Luke 2:8–14 in the spotlight, Linus tells Charlie Brown what Christmas is all about. His precious security blanket is dropped to the stage with "Fear not," as he begins the angel's announcement to the shepherds. Perhaps the creators of *A Charlie Brown Christmas* didn't intend to make a theological statement about the sufficiency of the gospel, but it seems fitting that Linus repeats the bit about "good tidings of great joy" without any other comfort, as if testifying to his cartoon friends and viewers alike that Jesus Christ is enough for him.

The good news the angel brings is "for all the people" (Luke 2:10), but the news of Jesus's birth appears to be nothing but "trouble" to Herod and the people of Jerusalem (see Matthew 2:3). Mary says that because of Jesus, the proud will be scattered and the mighty will be pulled down from their thrones (Luke 1:51–52)— not good news for these folks either. And at Jesus's dedication in the temple, Simeon prophesies that "this child is appointed for the fall and rising of many in Israel" (Luke 2:34).

Some three decades later, Jesus would say of himself, "Do not think that I have come to bring peace to the earth. I have not come to bring peace, but a sword" (Matthew 10:34). How then do we reconcile Jesus's own statement with the angel's announcement that His birth is good news for all people? In what sense can Linus drop his blanket—or any of us set aside our own trinkets of security, for that matter—with any real confidence, if Jesus has indeed come to earth with a sword in hand?

Christmas ought to be a reason for all people everywhere to rejoice, but it has become the great dividing line of history. The birth of Jesus inaugurated a new age in which God himself is bringing His kingdom to earth, a kingdom where all things will be made right. But those who belong to this world rail against such an announcement. They reveled and did what was right in their own eyes during the times of ignorance, but God says those days are now over (Acts 17:30). From the manger forward, as news of the Messiah reaches near and far, every man and woman must respond. Each of us must decide what to do with Jesus.

For devout Israelites who loved God, pored over His Word, and clung to His promises, the decision was easy. Simeon was such a man, having waited his entire life for "the consolation of Israel," for God to bring salvation to His people (Luke 2:25). Nearing death, he holds the baby Jesus in his arms and praises God for His faithfulness. But he knows the kingdom age being ushered in by the child will not bring consolation to everyone; it will reveal the unseen hearts of men and women as Jesus casts light into the darkest of places.

Simeon tells Mary that her baby, Jesus, will be "a sign that is opposed," and he warns her, "a sword will pierce through your own soul also" (Luke 2:34–35). Mary's soul will be pierced, as any mother's would, at the sight of her Son bloodied and struggling to breathe, hanging from a Roman cross. But it is for the cross that Jesus came (Mark 10:45). It is the cross that brings salvation. It is the cross that demands a response. And it is the cross that divides the world.

Of course, the world had been divided before Christ: There were Jews, and there were Gentiles. In the minds of most Jews, it was *Us versus Them*. The Jewish people looked for God to rescue them from the hands of their oppressors, whether those oppressors were the Egyptians, the Philistines, Babylonians, or the Romans, to name a few. It seems someone was always ready to oppose God's people. As the Jews understood human history, God was bringing a final act to the world stage, one in which Israel would be vindicated and her enemies devastated. But when Jesus the Messiah came, He didn't overthrow the Romans, and He didn't bring a political kingdom to the boundaries of the promised land. Instead, He willingly gave His life as a ransom for many—Jew and Gentile alike.

As a result, the world is now divided in a new way: between those who, by faith, accept Jesus's sacrifice on their behalf and those who think the cross is madness. Put another way, it is divided between those who submit to His lordship and those who reject the crucified King's claim to the throne. The apostle Paul writes, "I am not ashamed of the gospel, for it is the power of God for salvation to everyone who believes, to the Jew first and also to the Greek" (Romans 1:16). This is why the news of Christmas, the coming of King Jesus, is good news for all people. But elsewhere Paul says, "The word of the cross is folly to those who are perishing, but to us who are being saved it is the power of God" (1 Corinthians 1:18).

It is a mystery of divine grace. A mother cradles her baby before placing Him in a feeding-trough crib, and the world is changed forever. A humble Messiah must be approached humbly. Those who recognize Him do so. To them, He is known and loved. But the proud do not see a King at all. From the darkness, they squint, but all their eyes can glean is a peasant child in a manger and then a criminal on a cross.

Peace has come for those who will receive it, for "those with whom [God] is pleased" (Luke 2:14). For those who can recognize King Jesus, there is freedom. This world and all its entanglements— every security blanket of power, position, or possession—can be dropped to the stage, never to be picked up again.

8

When Answers to Prayers Collide

LUKE 1:5–25

"Do not be afraid, Zechariah, for your prayer has been heard, and your wife Elizabeth will bear you a son, and you shall call his name John."

—Luke 1:13

In the movie *It's a Wonderful Life*, the good-natured but wingless angel Clarence tells George Bailey, "Strange, isn't it? Each man's life touches so many other lives. When he isn't around he leaves an awful hole, doesn't he?" George has come to believe he is a failure—a nobody—and that his entire life hasn't amounted to much of anything. But then, after experiencing how the little town of Bedford Falls would be different if he had never been born, he comes to see, along with the audience watching the film, that his life has affected more people than he ever could have known. George Bailey isn't a nobody after all; he is a hero by means of the innumerable small but selfless things he's done, day in and day out. When you look back on a life lived that way, all those little kindnesses add up to a world of good.

George's dream had been to see exotic places, have adventures, and design great buildings that would survive long after he's gone. But each time it seemed he might have the opportunity to leave sleepy Bedford Falls, something came up. Time and again, George embraced personal disappointment for the good of the people around him. He gave up his world travels to assume his recently deceased father's spot at the head of the Bailey Building and Loan. Then he sacrificed his college career so his brother might have every opportunity available to him. And he even saved the meager family business (and arguably, the town) from a bank run with the money he had saved for an extended honeymoon. Each time he saw a need, George mustered the courage to postpone his dreams for the good of other people. But in my opinion, George Bailey isn't the only hero in the story.

The comfort of watching a movie like *It's a Wonderful Life* lies not in knowing there are good people like George Bailey in real life—or that you or I might be included in their number. Rather, we are heartened by seeing that if we are faithful, even life's biggest personal heartaches can be used for the good of the world. God is working behind the scenes, orchestrating events for the greatest good to those who love Him. He is the unnamed Actor in Bedford Falls, in your world, and in mine.

The Bible is full of George Baileys—imperfect people who struggle with life's disappointments, only to discover those heartaches are part of God's larger plan. Abraham and Sarah knew the sorrow of reaching old age without a child of their own. Joseph found himself a slave and in prison. David spent years on the run from a jealous king. Every day and in each moment of sadness and frustration, these men and women had to choose whether or not they would continue to trust the Lord.

Zechariah is such a man—a George Bailey—and it is with him that Luke begins his account of Jesus's birth. Both Zechariah and his wife, Elizabeth, are described as "righteous before God, walking blamelessly in all the commandments and statutes of the Lord" (1:6).

Zechariah and Elizabeth's disappointment is like Abraham and Sarah's before them: "They had no child, because Elizabeth was barren, and both were advanced in years" (1:7). But their disappointment is for a purpose; it will be used to bring God glory and to bring Israel the prophet God had promised would come to prepare the way for the Messiah.

The gospel of Jesus Christ is good news for anyone who has ever hung their head in sorrow for what might have been. It is the answer to every cry of *Why?* that resounds from the deepest recesses of our hearts—an answer that looks forward to the day when every tear will be wiped away and every wrong made right, when our disappointments will be swallowed up by the tide of God's overwhelming goodness.

When the angel Gabriel appears to Zechariah, it is to tell him God has heard his prayer. But there were, of course, two prayers on the lips of Zechariah. As he burned incense to the Lord in the temple, he offered up a prayer for the salvation and redemption of God's people. But in the years that passed before the fateful day when his name was chosen by lot, there were many days of waiting for a child. There can be no doubt that Zechariah pleaded with God for the blessing of hearing his wife, Elizabeth, say the words, "I'm pregnant!" and for the joy of holding a son or daughter in his aging arms.

I wonder if, as the years rolled by, Zechariah eventually stopped praying—if after reaching a certain age, he took the silence from heaven as the final answer to his prayers. Perhaps that explains why he doubted Gabriel's announcement that a son would be born to him. Maybe, to shield himself from pain, he had quarantined that section of his heart that could still imagine he might, one day, hear the cries of his child and offer the love he himself had received from so many years spent walking closely with God. After that divinely appointed day in the temple, as Zechariah spent the next nine months in silence—a consequence of his doubt—I wonder if he caught a glimpse of God's sense of humor: The man who didn't believe that God would speak in answer to his prayers was himself unable to speak.

In the birth of John the Baptist, Zechariah's prayer for the people of Israel collided with his prayer for a son to call his own. But this should not surprise us. After all, this is what the gospel promises to us—not that all our wants and desires will be fulfilled, but that "all things work together for good, for those who are called according to his purpose" (Romans 8:28). Christmas is a time when we have a reminder of this truth in every manger scene we view and in every Christmas card we write. God is at work behind the scenes so that no faithful George Bailey need wonder if his life is worth living, if his disappointments will be redeemed, or if there will ever come an answer to the deepest longings of his heart.

9

The Day John Met Jesus

LUKE 1:39–45

"For behold, when the sound of your greeting came to my ears, the baby in my womb leaped for joy."

—Luke 1:44

When Mary joined a group of other travelers leaving Nazareth for the hill country of Judah, she moved quickly. The angel Gabriel had said that her once barren cousin Elizabeth was expecting a child in her old age. If anyone would understand Mary's heart—the nervous wonder, the swirling questions—it would be Elizabeth. The journey from Galilee to Judea could take upward of three days, a trek that would become much more difficult in the coming months as her body changed with pregnancy. But at this early stage, and with the angel's words echoing in her ears, Mary made the trip.

She is not prepared for what she receives when she reaches her cousin's door. But given everything else she has experienced as of late, nothing should surprise her. Before Mary ever has a chance to share her news—the angel visit, the baby growing in her womb, or that He would be called "Son of the Most High" (Luke 1:32)—

Elizabeth interrupts: "Blessed are you among women, and blessed is the fruit of your womb!" (Luke 1:42). *How did she know?* Mary must have wondered. Luke tells us that at the sound of Mary's greeting, the Holy Spirit filled Elizabeth, and the still-forming baby John jumped for joy in her womb.

With the unborn Messiah's arrival, the Holy Spirit speaks words through Elizabeth that give Jesus glory. And with the coming of the King, John can't help but leap. These are signs that everything—absolutely everything—is about to change. From now on, Jesus's presence in the world will make all the difference. And it's all starting right here, in Zechariah and Elizabeth's home.

Nine months before Bethlehem, as Jesus's body is growing and forming in His mother's womb, while tiny lungs are developing and fingers and toes are waiting to sprout, He has already come. He is already Lord. (If there were ever a question about when life begins, this passage loudly declares that personhood begins at conception and that every unborn child has value in God's sight.) Elizabeth recognizes Jesus, but her perception is not due to some imagined glow from Mary or from any other external marker. As far as we can tell from the text of Luke, Mary is barely pregnant, showing no physical signs at all. It is Elizabeth's own son growing inside of her who draws her attention to Jesus, and it is the Holy Spirit who opens her eyes to see what can't be seen plainly.

This is a pattern that will continue throughout Jesus's earthly life. People who know Jesus—like John—will point to Him, draw attention to His presence, and declare that He is the Son of God. With physical eyes, people will see only the ordinary—a baby wrapped in cloths and lying in a manger, a carpenter walking along the shore with some fishermen, a rabbi eating with sinners, and a convict hanging from a Roman cross. As the Holy Spirit quickens the hearts and minds of men and women, they will come to see Jesus as He truly is—the promised Messiah who will save His people from their sins and set the world right. But to the rest of the world, the bright glory of the King comes wrapped in a dirty husk.

Isaiah provided a preview of this dirty-husk reality when he wrote, "He had no form or majesty that we should look at him, and no beauty that we should desire him" (Isaiah 53:2). And this is why John the Baptist was given to the world—to prepare the way for a King who would come without robes or crown. Some thirty years after this scene in Zechariah and Elizabeth's home, standing on the banks of the Jordan, John the Baptist will boldly proclaim, "Behold, the Lamb of God, who takes away the sin of the world!" (John 1:29). And with that call, those who have been given sight by the Holy Spirit will turn and follow Jesus. But John's mission began long before that day—even before the day of His birth—as he jumped within his mother's womb and announced the coming of the King.

Today, in many corners of our modern, politically correct world, there is outrage over Christmas. People are offended by the idea of a nativity display in public view, and they scoff if the cashier greets them with "Merry Christmas" instead of "Happy holidays." We enjoy the fun things of the season—the gifts, the lights, the eggnog lattés, and all the rest—but many would prefer a Christmas without Christ. That's because, just as it did two thousand years ago, the presence of Jesus demands a response.

Christmas is a reminder that Jesus reigns as King—right now. And it is a reminder that God sent His Son to save us from the guilt and weight of our sin—but that would mean we're guilty. If Christmas is true, then our world is radically out of step with God's kingdom, and our lives are profoundly out of order. Much needs to change. Things cannot go on as before. For those who cannot recognize Him, Jesus's presence at Christmas makes things awfully uncomfortable.

As an adult, John will stand up in the wilderness and speak to the crowds, shouting, "Do not begin to say to yourselves, 'We have Abraham as our father.' For I tell you, God is able from these stones to raise up children for Abraham" (Luke 3:8). Today he might shout, "Do not begin to say to yourselves, 'I'm better than most,' or 'There is nothing more to this world than what we can experience with our senses,' or 'Have you even seen my bank account?'" Any excuse will do, as long as it keeps the baby in the manger just a baby. Once He is more than a mere infant—once He is the King, once He is God—there is no getting around the confrontation of Christmas.

Advent is a time when we who know Jesus delight at His coming, as Elizabeth did, and we leap for joy with John. But it is also a time when many who would rather not think of Jesus at all are confronted by His presence. Amid the celebration and preparation, let's not forget to draw attention to Jesus as John did, making much of Him so our families, friends, and neighbors who do not yet know him might catch a glimpse of who He truly is. And let's not forget to pray that the Holy Spirit would speak deep within their hearts—places we cannot go—that many souls might be awakened to Jesus's presence and to the Savior's overwhelming love.

10

The Christmas Story According to Mark

MARK 1:1–11

And when he came up out of the water, immediately he saw the heavens being torn open and the Spirit descending on him like a dove.

—Mark 1:10

From the 1620s to the 1850s, Christmas was stolen in New England. In a culture that was unapologetically Christian and Protestant, the celebration of Jesus's birth that we call Christmas was shunned. The Grinch in this case was the Puritan community that had settled in the northeast corner of what is now the United States. These folks spurned the Christmas holiday because of its association with sometimes-sinful extravagance—eating and drinking to excess, dancing, and revelry.

The celebration of Christmas was actually against the law in Massachusetts from 1659 to 1681. The law specified that anyone "found observing, by abstinence from labor, feasting, or any other way, any such days as Christmas day" would be forced to pay five shillings for each offense. December 25 had been the date of the Roman holiday Saturnalia, and so it was thought that any commemoration on that day would smack of pagan ritual.

But the Christmas-killing argument to end all arguments for the Puritans came from Scripture itself, or rather, from what cannot be found there: God's Word never commands Christ's followers to honor His birthday. The Puritans reasoned, *Who are we to invent a holiday for God?* So Christmas was removed from the calendar. The light emanating to the rest of the world from the "city on a hill" in old New England was decidedly not a twinkly Christmas light.

While there's much to commend in the Puritan approach to Bible application, the apostle Paul seems to take a different tack when it comes to celebrations of God's goodness. Paul writes to the Colossians, "*Whatever you do*, in word or deed, do everything in the name of the Lord Jesus, giving thanks to God the Father through him" (Colossians 3:17; emphasis added). And to the Corinthians, he says, "So whether you eat or drink, or *whatever you do*, do all to the glory of God" (1 Corinthians 10:31; emphasis added). Paul's words don't give us license to do anything we want, but they do free us to celebrate goodness wherever we find it. Still, I think that in one sense, the Puritans were on to something: We should never limit our thinking about Jesus's coming to earth to a single day of the year. Even if we don't share a big meal, exchange presents, or put a tinsel-strewn evergreen in the living room, our lives should reflect the truth of Christmas—God coming in the flesh—all year long.

The four gospels were written to encourage people to follow Jesus. Matthew, Mark, Luke, and John each tell the story of His life, death, and resurrection, though with admittedly different perspectives and goals for their writing. But while Matthew and Luke each give us their own account of Jesus's birth, and John gives us a glimpse into the eternal, heavenly life of Christ prior to the first Christmas, Mark appears silent on the subject. Like those New England Puritans, he seems content to leave Christmas out altogether. Or could it be that Mark is prompting his readers to lead lives that reflect the truth of Christmas with what *is* included in the opening of his gospel?

True enough. There are no angels, no wise men, and no manger in Mark's gospel. Instead, Mark sets the stage by referring to "the beginning of the gospel of Jesus Christ" (1:1). With such an opening, we might expect him to begin in Bethlehem, or in Nazareth with Mary and Joseph, or even in heaven with the Word who was with God and who was God (John 1:1). Instead, Mark starts with prophecies about John the Baptist from the Old Testament writings of Malachi and Isaiah. He begins his account of Jesus's earthly life on the shores of the Jordan River.

Though Israel's prophets describe many of the elements we later find in the birth narratives—Bethlehem, the virgin birth, Jesus's Davidic lineage—the Old Testament closes not with one of these but with a prediction about John the Baptist. The Lord says in Malachi, "Behold, I will send you Elijah the prophet before the great and awesome day of the LORD comes" (4:5). And Mark makes it clear that John is the one sent in the spirit and power of Elijah, mentioning John's clothes of camel's hair and his leather belt, a tribute to Elijah's famous wardrobe (1:6; compare 2 Kings 1:8). Mark picks up the story of redemption here, rather than in Bethlehem. But I believe he still has Christmas in full view.

As the scene unfolds at the Jordan, John baptizes Jesus. And when Jesus comes up out of the water, God the Father speaks through the clouds, and the Holy Spirit, like a dove, descends on the Lord. All four gospels record the account in one form or another, but there's an extra detail—an extra word—unique to Mark. And it's in that word that we find a Christmas clue.

Mark says, "And when [Jesus] came up out of the water, immediately he saw the heavens being torn open and the Spirit descending on him like a dove" (1:10). All of the other gospel writers mention heaven opening and the Spirit descending, but it is only Mark who tells us that heaven was *torn* open, painting a picture not easily forgotten. And it's one that would have been familiar to Mark's original readers because they would have come across it before. Toward the end of Isaiah, we read, "Oh, that You would tear open the heavens and come down, that the mountains would quake at Your presence" (64:1 NASB). The prophet Isaiah, writing about the nation of Judah in captivity in Babylon, implores the Lord to intercede—to tear apart the veil between heaven and earth and step down into history. At Christmas, that's precisely what happened.

Mark isn't ignoring the events of the first Christmas; he's pointing out what those events mean. When God tore open the heavens and came down to earth, it wasn't in the way Isaiah had asked. Mountains didn't tremble, and evil was not destroyed in a single day. Instead, there was a teenage virgin and a manger and some shepherds. But God's kingdom came to earth all the same, and because of Jesus's perfect life and His perfect sacrifice on our behalf, evil's days are numbered. This is the story Mark is about to tell in his gospel—how God's kingdom is invading earth—and he's inviting his readers to live in the light of this reality, to live in the light of Christmas, right from the start.

11

The First Christmas Carol

LUKE 1:46–55

"For behold, from now on all generations will call me blessed."
—Luke 1:48

On Christmas Eve many years ago, my dad decided to paint the garage—at least that's what he told my sister and me. He cautioned us not to go anywhere near that part of the house while he worked—and that's all he needed to say to us. I was just five years old, so I took my father's stern warning seriously. I imagined that we would be instantly covered in paint simply by opening the door, or perhaps we would pass out from the fumes with just a whiff.

A few hours later, my sister's eight-year-old friend, who lived down the road (and who was a little more streetwise than my sister and me), clued us in to the dubious nature of my father's claim. "It's Christmas Eve; there's no way he's painting. There must be presents in there—something big," she said with the conviction of a seasoned skeptic. *A near life-size Millennium Falcon from* Star Wars? I wondered. *A mountain of Legos perhaps?* My mind raced with excitement. So the three of us risked certain death from paint inhalation to sneak a peek at untold toy treasures.

Under a big, white sheet we found new bicycles assembled by my dad that morning—one for me (with training wheels) and one for my sister. Both were blue with white tassels on the handlebars and chrome accents that glistened in the early afternoon sunshine we had let sneak in with us through the open door.

On Christmas morning, we offered up Oscar-worthy performances of surprise. Mom and Dad never would have known about our unauthorized Christmas Eve preview if it hadn't been for our partner in crime—my sister's best friend from down the street—who spilled the beans later that day. My mother asked her what she thought of our new bikes, and without a second thought to her betrayal, she blurted, "They're great. I liked them yesterday when we saw them in the garage."

Some people think that finding your presents early takes the fun out of Christmas. To a certain extent, they may be right. But as I went to bed on Christmas Eve, knowing full well what would be under the tree the next morning, I was still very excited. I had, of course, robbed my parents of seeing a genuine look of surprise on my face, and I had traded in the excitement of the unknown for the excitement of looking ahead to something certain and good.

This sort of exchange happened for Mary when the angel Gabriel appeared to her over two thousand years ago. Like every other faithful Jew, Mary had been looking forward to God acting in history to set His people—and even the world—free from the tyranny of sin, demonic power, and injustice. God had given some clues about how this would take place, but until Gabriel told this teenaged bride-to-be about the divine child who would be born to her in the coming months, no one quite knew how God would do it.

When we reach the section of Luke's gospel that contains Mary's song (Luke 1:46–55), often called the "Magnificat" (a title derived from the Latin translation of the song's first line), our ears are filled with the praises of a young woman who has come to feel the excitement of expectation. God is coming—and has already arrived—as a child growing in her womb. Every promise God made to His people down through the centuries will now come true in Him! Mary recounts how God had saved His people in the past, and she looks forward to what God will now do through the Son who will be born to her:

> He has shown strength with his arm; he has scattered the proud in the thoughts of their hearts; he has brought down the mighty from their thrones and exalted those of humble estate; he has filled the hungry with good things, and the rich he has sent away empty. He has helped his servant Israel, in remembrance of his mercy, as he spoke to our fathers, to Abraham and to his offspring forever. (Luke 1:51–55)

For those of us who stand on the other side of the cross reading her words today, there is a bittersweet flavor to the song on our lips. The rich and powerful still do as they please, God's people still have their enemies, and the hungry are still left wanting. These many years later, all has not been made right with the world. Not yet anyway.

In the middle of the Christmas story, the Magnificat is a reminder that we, like Mary, are still waiting for God to bring final justice—to put the nail in the coffin of all that is wrong on planet Earth. Our world today is not all that different than it was in Mary's day. The people have changed, the national boundaries fall in different places, and technology has made many parts of life easier (while confounding others); but sin, death, and injustice still take their toll.

As Mary sings her song, a few miles away in Jerusalem Herod sits on his throne. This same Herod will order the murder of infants and toddlers in Bethlehem in a misguided attempt to kill Jesus. He may enjoy the title "king," but Herod is really only a tool of the Roman Empire. Israel is not free; her people are slaves to the world's superpower—a vicious, unrelenting nation of idol worshippers who see the promised land as just another backwater province, nothing more than a truck stop between Egypt and Asia Minor. But Mary doesn't flinch. She knows that God is good, even while the brokenness of her world screams otherwise.

Mary's song of praise does not wait for the world to be made right. She is bursting with joy because of who God is and what He had done for Israel in generations past. While the world would view Mary's pregnancy as a curse—she is betrothed, but the child does not belong to her bridegroom—she knows it is a blessing.

Mary has a lot to teach me. Too often I'm more comfortable withholding praise until I get a peek at what's hidden in the garage. I want to see God at work; I want to see results. When I am faced with uncertainty and the road ahead looks uncomfortable, God's goodness is not the first thing I look for.

At Christmas, God stepped into history to undo the curse of sin and death—to put right everything that has gone wrong. Like Mary, we look forward to the day when all things will be made new and every tear will be wiped away. But in Jesus, God has spoken. The price has been paid, and the kingdom of heaven advances. We can have confidence that evil's days are numbered. We, like Mary, can sing God's praises, knowing we are indeed blessed no matter where we find ourselves—not because the brokenness of this world screams any less loudly than it did in her day, but because God is still good.

12

The Familiar Voice in a Baby's Cry

LUKE 1:57–80

"And you, child, will be called the prophet of the Most High; for you will go before the Lord to prepare his ways."

—Luke 1:76

When I was growing up, our family always spent the day after Thanksgiving at Jones Family Farms in Shelton, Connecticut. Every year, we'd drive out to the farm, take a short, tractor-driven hayride, and walk for what seemed like hours to find the perfect Christmas tree. And when the classic American tree had been found, bound, and loaded atop our family's Volvo wagon, we'd have hot cider and cookies around a campfire. As I grew older, this Christmas tree run seemed more like a chore than a fun day out with my family. Like most teenagers, I loathed scheduled family time, especially doing something as cliché as cutting down a Christmas tree. But as an adult, now with a family of my own, I look back on those days spent at Jones with a sense of nostalgia.

We live in Tennessee now, so I can't go back to that tree farm in Connecticut every year on the Friday after Thanksgiving. That tradition was dead—or so I thought. A few years ago, however, my brother, James, told me about a Christmas tree farm he had discovered about thirty miles from where we lived at the time, which was in Georgia. It had the same rolling hills full of evergreens, the same tractors offering hayrides, and even cookies and cider around a campfire. And when James got the chance to talk with the owner, he found out the most incredible thing: Jones Family Farms—that same farm more than eight hundred miles to the north that had become a part of our Christmas traditions growing up—served as the inspiration for this tree farm in the North Georgia hills.

So my brother and I could carry on our childhood tradition with our families in tow, venturing out on the day after Thanksgiving to cut down a Christmas tree. And each time we did that, we lived out a story we want retold every year. We remembered Christmases past and added to our collection of memories. Our Christmases were not always easy growing up; some of them were downright painful. But when we were trudging a path together to find the perfect tree, those bad memories lost their grip, and the good and funny times settled in the forefronts of our minds. This is the power of a story retold. This is the power of living out a good memory. It is something like this that's at work as Luke recounts the story of John the Baptist's birth, weaving together familiar Old Testament threads to show that John's role in the story of redemption will make a way for the fulfillment of all God's promises.

It's hard to read the account of God giving a son to barren Elizabeth and Zechariah without also thinking of Hannah, the Old Testament saint to whom God gave Samuel. She too was barren. Hannah prayed to God at the tabernacle, and Zechariah prays in the temple. Both were given sons who would be set apart for service to the Lord, and both sons would prepare the way for a coming king. Since the time of Samuel, pain and disappointment had run their course through Israel's sordid history. The people had broken their covenant with God again and again, failing to reflect His glory. They had lost their freedom to invading armies more than once, and control of their land passed between world powers uninterrupted, with each new oppressor more insidious than the last. But the story of Samuel was a bright spot in Israel's story. God had done wonderful things through that prophet's life. And now, as the story of John the Baptist begins to unfold, it seems God is about to do something wonderful again.

Samuel led the people of Israel through a turbulent time—out of the period of the judges, when "everyone did what was right in his own eyes" (Judges 17:6), through the tumultuous reign of Saul, to the selection of his successor, David, a man after God's own heart (1 Samuel 13:14). David's reign was a golden age, the high-water mark for the people of Israel. Samuel was the one who anointed David and who prepared the way for the coming king. At a sacrifice in Bethlehem, surrounded by David's father and brothers, Samuel poured oil over David's head, setting him apart as the future king over the struggling nation.

More than a thousand years later, in the Jordan River, surrounded by crowds, John would baptize Jesus with water, anointing Him the Messiah—the King who would sit upon David's throne forever. God would speak from heaven, confirming what had just taken place: "You are my beloved Son; with you I am well pleased" (Luke 3:22; compare Psalm 2:7; Isaiah 42:1).

John's birth story also contains an Elijah thread, seen most notably in the words of Gabriel, who tells Zechariah that John "will go before [the Lord] in the spirit and power of Elijah" (Luke 1:17). Elijah was among the very small remnant of the faithful during a time when Israel had turned to the dark power of false gods. Elijah called the people of God to repentance (1 Kings 18:21), confronted the prophets of Baal (1 Kings 18:20–40), denounced the actions of the corrupt King Ahab (1 Kings 18:18), and provoked murderous rage in Ahab's wife, Jezebel (1 Kings 19:2). In the same manner, John the Baptist would call the people of his day to repentance (Luke 3:3). He would confront false religious leaders (Matthew 3:7), denounce the actions of Herod the tetrarch (Luke 3:19), and provoke murderous rage in Herod's wife, Herodias (Mark 6:18–19).

God had used the prophetic voice of Elijah to call His people back to faith, and so through John, God would once again call His people back, imploring them to turn from their idols.

The account of John's birth is already a crash course in Old Testament history, but there is yet another thread from Israel's past winding its way through John's life, tucked away in his family tree: "There was a priest named Zechariah, of the division of Abijah. And he had a wife from the daughters of Aaron, and her name was Elizabeth" (Luke 1:5). Luke is making it clear that John is from the line of the high priest—on both sides of the family. As a young man, he would identify the Lamb of God (John 1:29) and wash the ultimate sacrifice (Luke 3:21), and in doing so, he would fulfill his priestly duties.

Each of these ancient threads—Samuel, Elijah, and Aaron—reveals something of the way John would prepare the way for Jesus. As a judge like Samuel, he would anoint the King. As a prophet like Elijah, he would call the people of promise back to their God. And as a priest like Aaron, he would prepare the sacrifice that removes sin. But there is another way in which John would fulfill his father's prophetic words to "go before the Lord to prepare his ways" (Luke 1:76): John would die. The Gospels record that John was beheaded as a party favor at the request of a teenager (Luke 9:9; Mark 6:14–29). It seems fitting that the forerunner of a crucified King would himself be killed. John's life is cut short to mark the path the Messiah will take.

The strands of Old Testament history woven into Luke's narrative of John's birth are meant to remind us of God's faithfulness to Israel. The gospel is the final chapter to every unfinished story from Genesis through Malachi, and that chapter begins with Christmas. So there are two babies in the Christmas story—Jesus, to answer the longing of every broken heart, and John, to prepare those broken hearts to recognize their King, all the while echoing the familiar refrain of God's voice down through history.

13

The New Creation and the Old, Old Story

JOHN 1:1–18

And the Word became flesh and dwelt among us, and we have seen his glory, glory as of the only Son from the Father, full of grace and truth.

—John 1:14

Celebrating Christmas can be dangerous. If we're not careful, we can start to think the whole thing is about Jesus being born in Bethlehem, about good news of great joy, and about God having "moved into the neighborhood," as Eugene Peterson so thoughtfully put it (John 1:14 MSG). In one sense, Christmas *is* about all those things—and it would be a tragedy if we were to forget these truths or take them for granted. But in our efforts to shoo away Santa Claus and repel the commercialism of the season, we run the risk of focusing so intently on the manger that our eyes go crossed and we lose the point of it all. Jesus *is* the point of it all, but the Christmas story is about so much more than His birth. Advent is but the turning point in a beautifully crafted, wonderfully true story—a masterpiece God himself has been writing for a very long time—since the beginning of all things.

In the opening pages of her bestselling children's book *The Jesus Storybook Bible*, Sally Lloyd-Jones tells her young readers (and their parents and grandparents) what to expect from the Bible:

> There are lots of stories in the Bible, but all the stories are telling one Big Story. The Story of how God loves his children and comes to rescue them. It takes the whole Bible to tell this Story. And at the center of the Story, there is a baby. Every Story in the Bible whispers his name. He is like the missing piece in a puzzle—the piece that makes all the other pieces fit together, and suddenly you can see a beautiful picture.[1]

For many Christmas seasons now, Laurin and I have had the privilege of hearing these words read aloud in Lloyd-Jones's own wonderfully charming British voice. Every year, we attend a Christmas concert at the Ryman Auditorium in Nashville, where Sally Lloyd-Jones kicks off the show with a reading from *The Jesus Storybook Bible*.

The concert itself is strange among holiday concerts. No Santa Claus. No "Jingle Bells." No holiday sweaters. Instead, Andrew Peterson and a gaggle of musicians, singers, storytellers, and songwriters gather together to perform *Behold the Lamb of God*, a concept album Peterson dreamed up to tell what he calls, "the true tall tale of the coming of Christ." Beginning with Israel's early history in Egyptian slavery, the songs in the show progress through the Old Testament to arrive at the manger in Bethlehem. To be sure, the story Peterson tells could begin earlier—with Abraham, or perhaps with Noah, or with Adam and Eve in the garden—but his point in telling the Christmas story in this way remains: Christmas was never meant to be cut off from the larger story of redemption.

Andrew Peterson and Sally Lloyd-Jones have hit upon something critical to helping us understand the significance of Jesus's identity, and therefore the significance of His birth. The apostle John, in his gospel, is concerned with readers discovering who Jesus really is, so he tells the Christmas story from a view entirely different from those of the other evangelists. He looks back to a time before Bethlehem, before Israel, and even before the garden.

John starts his gospel with, "In the beginning," undoubtedly a conscious reprise of the very first phrase in the book of Genesis. "In the beginning was the Word, and the Word was with God, and the Word was God," he writes (1:1). John echoes Genesis in order to retell the story of creation and show that Jesus, and Christmas, were no mere afterthoughts in the mind of the Father. Jesus was with God in the beginning, and in the unfathomable mystery of the Trinity, is himself God.

When God spoke creation into being, He did not merely speak words created out of nothing; God himself—Christ Jesus—was the Word. "All things were made through him, and without him was not any thing made that was made" (John 1:3). And when the Word Jesus Christ went forth from God, His creation project was begun.

But John doesn't stop there. He tells his readers the Word has gone out again in His day: "The Word became flesh and dwelt among us," he says (1:14). When God sends forth His Word, creation happens. And when God sent Jesus to earth that first Christmas, a new creation project was begun. With His coming, "the light shines in the darkness" (1:5), just as it did in Genesis. A new age dawned. This is the weight of Christ's birth: God is making all things new.

But when God creates something new, He is not like a child who, unhappy with his castle of blocks, knocks the whole thing down and starts over. To the child, the first castle doesn't matter; it may as well never have existed. But God loves His first creation; it matters to Him. So even with its unyielding decay and its unrelenting climate of violence and pain, God chooses to redeem this world and rescue its people who call on His name. The new creation that began the first Christmas, then, is not a do-over. Rather, it's the unfolding of a plan set in motion by God long ago, and the gospel accounts of Jesus's life, death, and resurrection are but the climax to a story God began telling long ago in the book of Genesis—all the way back at the beginning.

You and I are a part of that story too. When we celebrate Christmas, we celebrate the new creation that is breaking in all around us as God's kingdom takes new territory in our world. We can look forward to the day when Jesus will return to fully and finally set the world right. That is the point of Christmas. And that is the story God is writing.

Too easily I forget that God is still writing His story and that my life is a part of it—just as Abraham's life was, and Hannah's, and Elijah's, and the lives of all the other faithful men and women in the Bible we consider altogether different from our own. But maybe we're not so different from these folks. "These all died in faith," says the writer of Hebrews, "not having received the things promised, but having seen them and greeted them from afar" (11:13). While we stand on the far side of some of those promises coming true in Jesus—on the other side of Christmas and Easter—there are other promises yet to be fulfilled. So we stand together with our spiritual ancestors to greet those promises from afar, and we too must play our parts in the story God is writing. When we celebrate Christmas, we remember God's faithfulness to past generations and to our own, and we join with the saints who have gone before us in affirming that His story is the best of stories.

John's prologue connects Christmas with the cosmic purposes of our Creator. The first eighteen verses of his gospel make the audacious claim that Jesus is eternal God, insisting God loves us so much that He became one of us and entered into the very masterwork He is writing—a story of redemption, rescue, and re-creation. Christmas is about nothing less than the Son of God coming to earth as a baby, and because it is about nothing less than that, it is also about so much more.

A Christmas Engagement Story

JOHN 14:1–7

"And if I go and prepare a place for you, I will come again and will take you to myself, that where I am you may be also."

—John 14:3

Rose petals were strewn along the path from her foyer to her living room, and the end of the trail was lit with dozens of candles. But her eyes were drawn to the center of the room, where a ball of mistletoe was suspended from the ceiling with red ribbon. Taking Laurin by the hand, I guided her down the rosy walkway and retrieved a small box dangling from the kissing ball. Inside was a diamond ring, an expensive but relatively small token of the commitment I was about to make. I got down on one knee and told Laurin how much I loved her heart. I told her I didn't want to spend another Christmas apart from her for the rest of my life. And then I asked her to marry me.

That was Christmas Eve in 2012. Now that kissing ball hangs from the ceiling in our living room each year during the holidays as a reminder of our Christmas engagement. But as it turns out,

Christmas itself is already an engagement reminder. It's when Jesus made an engagement promise of His own.

In ancient Jewish culture, the initial commitment of marriage had two stages, beginning with betrothal and ending with consummation and celebration. Although today we tend to think of the engagement period as bearing less commitment than the wedding day, betrothal in first-century Israel was as binding as marriage. (That's why, for example, Joseph planned to divorce Mary when he thought she had been unfaithful. Because they were already considered legally married, it would not have been enough to simply call off the wedding; see Matthew 1:19.)

Betrothal was serious business and was not to be taken lightly. It began when a man visited the father of his potential bride and asked for permission to marry his daughter. If the father gave his consent, the two signed a contract and the bridegroom paid an agreed-upon price for his bride. At this point, the marriage officially began, although the couple would not live together as husband and wife or consummate the marriage physically for some time.

Once the bride and groom were betrothed, they started preparing for life together. The bride made herself ready for the day of her beloved's return, while the groom built a place for them to live, usually as an addition onto his father's home. This preparation time could last a year or more, after which the groom would once again visit the father of the bride's home—this time with friends and witnesses in tow. The marriage was then consummated in a special room while the bridesmaids, the best man, and witnesses all waited outside. Afterward, this collected group of friends returned to the home of the groom's father for a weeklong celebration.

At Christmas, Jesus began His earthly life, His visit to the home of His bride. The purpose of His visit was to pay the necessary price—His own blood, poured out on the cross. In giving instructions about marriage, Paul says this about Jesus's sacrifice:

> Husbands, love your wives, as Christ loved the church and gave himself up for her, that he might sanctify her, having cleansed her by the washing of water with the word, so that he might present the church to himself in splendor, without spot or wrinkle or any such thing, that she might be holy and without blemish. (Ephesians 5:25–27)

The purpose for the cross was that Jesus might present the church to himself on the day of the heavenly wedding feast in the age to come. Death was the price Jesus paid in order to marry His bride. And by paying that price, Jesus was making a promise to come back for her.

After the covenant was ratified and payment made, like any honorable bridegroom, Jesus went to prepare a place for His bride in His Father's house. As He told His disciples, "In my Father's house are many rooms. If it were not so, would I have told you that I go to prepare a place for you?" (John 14:2). And because of all that Jesus did, that's where we find ourselves in the grandest of all wedding stories—waiting for Christ's return, so we can be with Him forever and the celebration can begin.

Without Christmas, there would be no Good Friday. Without Good Friday, there would be no Easter. And without Easter, there would be no looking forward to the Lord's second coming. At Christmas, Jesus set the future in motion. And each year, we have a reminder of Jesus's visit, a reminder of the payment He made on the cross, and a reminder of His promise to return.

15

The Nightmare after Christmas

MATTHEW 2:13–17

Then Herod, when he saw that he had been tricked by the wise men, became furious, and he sent and killed all the male children in Bethlehem and in all the region who were two years old or under, according to the time that he had ascertained from the wise men.

—Matthew 2:16

During the winter of 1914, five months deep into World War I, an unofficial ceasefire settled in small pockets along the Western Front. A few weeks earlier, Pope Benedict XV had suggested a temporary truce for the Christmas holiday, but the commanding officers on both sides rejected the idea. On Christmas Eve, however, German and Allied soldiers alike followed the pope's counsel and began singing Christmas carols together across the battle lines. The next morning, German soldiers greeted Allied troops, wished them "Merry Christmas," and offered gifts of cigarettes and rations. It was even reported that in one spot a friendly soccer match was played that Christmas afternoon.

This story wouldn't make sense if it took place at any other time of year, but somehow at Christmas it seems right that the world be a place of "peace, good will toward men" (Luke 2:14 KJV). We all want Christmas to be special—a day of magic even—when heaven really does seem to invade our world. We long for the kind of Christmas many of us remember from childhood or for the kind of Christmas we wish we'd had. But too often, December 25 is just like any other day here on planet Earth. Loved ones still die, hearts are still broken, and sin still takes its toll. No break is taken from the battles we wage, so when hardships find us at Christmas, life seems especially sharp and cruel. Heaven may have begun its incursion into our broken world the day Jesus was born, but the world remains broken all the same, groaning with longing for its final redemption.

Shortly after Jesus's birth, a gruesome and almost unthinkable crime was committed. It's so terrible that Luke doesn't even mention it in his account.[2] What we know comes from Matthew. He tells us that when the wise men left Herod's court, Herod gave them instructions to return with details about the newborn King so he too could worship (2:8). Of course it was never his intention to bow down before a baby; his plans were more diabolical. And when the magi didn't return as he had expected, he widened his target. Herod the Great ordered the murder of every male child two years of age or younger in Bethlehem and the surrounding area (2:16).

There are no easy answers to the questions that fill our minds when we read this account, including the most basic of all: *Why would God allow this, especially at a time bubbling over with hope and expectation?* God knew Herod would take these children's lives; He even sent an angel to warn Joseph in a dream. But it seems there was no warning issued to the other families in Bethlehem that night. Nothing was done to stop the wrath of the tyrant-king. Nothing was done to keep the children safe.

In commenting on this passage, Bible scholars will often show how Matthew used this episode to accentuate the parallels between

Moses, God's deliverer in the Old Testament, and Jesus, His deliverer in the New. Just as baby Moses had been rescued in the midst of a deadly plot from Pharaoh, Jesus is saved under similar circumstances. While that explanation may satisfy literary curiosities, it hardly addresses our hearts' deepest questions. The Word of God isn't a novel. Every word is true. Regardless of how much symmetry we may find in the Bible's pages, this scene is still difficult to take in.

This side of heaven, we're not likely to fully understand why God allowed such a malicious act to punch holes in Bethlehem's peaceful night air. The problem of evil is as old as sin itself, and God, in His wisdom, has not given us answers to all our questions (see Job 38–41), but there is a difference between not having the answer to a question and a question not having an answer. For now, we must rest in the knowledge that "for those who love God all things work together for good" (Romans 8:28). I realize it seems vulgar to talk of goodness coming from acts of terror, but that is the audacious hope of the gospel. God's goodness answers the problem of evil at the most fundamental level.

We don't know precisely how God will make something good out of the sin of Herod and his soldiers. That is the reason that, from our perspective, acts like these seem senseless and indiscriminate. But we have God's promise that "all things," including this horrific act, will bring about goodness, and we have examples from Scripture to show how God has used sin and wickedness for good in the past. Think about Joseph, sold into slavery by his brothers, only to rise up and save the lives of many people, including those same brothers (Genesis 50:20). And then there's Solomon, the product of David's marriage to Bathsheba—a union that began with adultery, murder, and lies. It was during Solomon's reign that Israel enjoyed an unprecedented time of peace and prosperity, and it was through Solomon's pen that the Bible gained many of its celebrated expressions of wisdom. But the greatest example of God turning evil to good is seen in the murder of His own Son. Jesus was "crucified and killed by the hands of lawless men" (Acts 2:23), yet in the purposes of God, Christ's death meant blessing for all who would put their trust in Him.

These examples offer little consolation to the mothers and fathers of Bethlehem who ached and wailed at the loss of their children, and they offer little solace to those who mourn in the aftermath of tragedy today. Without careful reflection, it can appear that, through His promises, God is calling "good" that which is evil, as if the message of Scripture were simply about finding the silver lining to every gray cloud. Sin is sin, and evil is evil—and God hates both. This is why God sent His Son in the first place: to put an end to the curse of sin. At the cross, Jesus paid sin's penalty, and when He returns, He'll destroy evil for good.

The Bible tells us that in the final chapter of the story He is writing, "[God] will wipe away every tear from their eyes, and death shall be no more, neither shall there be mourning, nor crying, nor pain anymore, for the former things have passed away" (Revelation 21:4). In the end, there will be more than a temporary ceasefire to give us a break from our heartache. The battle lines will be forever erased. Evil will be swallowed up by goodness once and for all.

16

Caesar, the Census, and the Coming of Christ

LUKE 2:1–7

And Joseph also went up from Galilee, from the town of Nazareth, to Judea, to the city of David, which is called Bethlehem, because he was of the house and lineage of David, to be registered with Mary, his betrothed, who was with child.

—Luke 2:4–5

The temperature outside hovered around five below zero, and the wind whipped through the streets of Chicago, making my already cold face truly frigid. I pushed through the revolving door, stomped snow off my shoes and onto the welcome mat, and then headed to the hotel's front desk, suitcase in hand. It was after midnight, so there was no one waiting to receive late arrivals. I pressed down on the bell and released a louder-than-expected chime that echoed through the lobby. Within seconds, a woman with a warm smile appeared from around the corner and welcomed me to the Windy City.

I gave her my name, my credit card, and the usual information needed to check in. While she was clicking at her keyboard, she asked me how my trip had been. "Actually," I replied, "it was pretty awful." And then I explained: "My flight was delayed three hours because of the snowstorm, and then I discovered that my luggage hadn't arrived with my plane, so I had to wait for it at O'Hare. And because I was late, I missed the last shuttle to your hotel and had to get a cab. Oh—and I spilled coffee on my lap this morning at Starbucks, so I've had an awkward brown stain on my pants all day."

The woman behind the counter—Angie, according to her name tag—smiled, somewhat amused by my tale of woe but also with genuine warmth. "Well, I hope your trip gets better from here," she said as she handed me the keycard for my room and directed me to the elevators.

When I got to my assigned room and opened the door, I was shocked. I had only booked a double bed for the night—no frills, no extras. I was in town on business, and my company didn't treat splurging too kindly. But there in front of me was the biggest hotel room I had ever seen: a master suite with a sunken living room, a library, two bathrooms, a hot tub, an aquarium filled with exotic fish, a balcony overlooking Lake Michigan, and even a private sauna. I put my suitcase and coat down on the king-size bed and made my way back to the hotel lobby to thank Angie, but she had gone home for the night. Her replacement for the evening told me she'd been known to bless people with a surprise upgrade every now and then, especially when it looked like someone could use a blessing.

On the elevator ride back up to my incredible room, I thought about timing. All day long, I had considered myself behind schedule. A storm had dumped a foot of snow on my plans, and I grumbled against the inconvenience of it all. But if it hadn't snowed and my flight hadn't been delayed, I would have arrived at the hotel on time—before Angie's shift and without my story of frustration. I wondered if God smiled as He watched me chasing after wind all day, knowing what was waiting for me in Chicago. I imagined His smile might have looked like the one Angie had on her face as she handed me my room key that evening.

The Bible doesn't tell us what was going through the minds of Joseph and Mary as they left Nazareth for Bethlehem, but I bet they were fascinated with the timing of it all. They had been told months before that the baby growing inside Mary's womb was the Christ, and as they remembered the Scriptures that foretold His coming, I wonder if they stumbled over this little prophecy in Micah: "But you, O Bethlehem Ephrathah, who are too little to be among the clans of Judah, from you shall come forth for me one who is to be ruler in Israel, whose coming forth is from of old, from ancient days" (5:2). The Messiah was to come from Bethlehem, not Nazareth. Perhaps Joseph contemplated "helping" God by taking His bride to Bethlehem for no other reason than to make the prophecy true, but that might have seemed like cheating. And then one day, he was notified of Caesar's census. He would be required to travel to his ancestral home—the town of Bethlehem—in order to register. God had planned these details long ago, and everything was moving along, right on schedule.

The Bible also doesn't tell us what Caesar Augustus was thinking when he issued his decree, but I imagine it was quite the power trip to place his seal on an edict that would make the entire world stand up and be counted—and travel for days and weeks to do so. I'm sure he had no thought at all about a Jewish carpenter and his pregnant wife being displaced by the census, and I'm sure he had never heard of Micah's prophecy or that the King of the Jews was to be born in Bethlehem. His only concern was maximizing tax revenue—counting the empire's people and property—so Rome could prosper. I'm quite sure Caesar, the most powerful man in the world, had no idea that he was but a pawn in the hand of God.

As we read Luke's gospel, we can see this invisible hand of God at work in a way that Caesar never could. The timing of the census is no mere coincidence, and the location of Jesus's birth, no mere accident. God orchestrates events to bring about His purposes.

Jesus is born in Bethlehem because it is David's town—and Jesus is the King who will sit on David's throne forever (Daniel 2:44; compare Luke 1:32–33).

Have you ever thought about the inconvenience of it all? Joseph and Mary had to travel for days to reach Bethlehem. They were uncomfortable days, on foot or by donkey, and perhaps in the late stages of Mary's pregnancy. No air conditioning. No GPS. No rest stops. When they arrived in Judea, they found Bethlehem crowded; it was so packed that the home in which they were to stay had no guest room available. And then there's everyone else in the Roman world to consider. The census required every male citizen to return to his family's city of origin. That meant thousands upon thousands of pilgrimages at great personal expense and sometimes hardship. Things would have been a lot simpler if Jesus could have been born in Nazareth or if Joseph and Mary had lived in Bethlehem to begin with.

But the events of the first Christmas unfold the way God had ordained, "when the fullness of time had come" (Galatians 4:4). The census decree was not a necessary corrective measure applied to get the story back on track; it was part of God's plan all along. Although to any onlooker, Joseph and Mary would have seemed like typical Jewish peasants in the crowds, their soon-to-be-born Son was the one the entire nation of Israel was waiting for—and the one the rest of mankind didn't even know they should be waiting for. The entire world was unsettled so He could be born at just the right moment and at just the right place. To every person forced to travel and register, the census appeared to be nothing but trouble—a terrible distraction from the business of real life. Still, I wonder if God smiled as He thought about the indescribable blessing the world was about to receive as He gave it His Son.

17

The Gospel and the Other "Virgin" Birth

ISAIAH 7:10–17; MATTHEW 1:22–23

All this took place to fulfill what the Lord had spoken by the prophet: "Behold, the virgin shall conceive and bear a son, and they shall call his name Immanuel."

—Matthew 1:22–23

The late talk show host Larry King was once asked whom, from all of history, he'd like the chance to interview. He responded, "Jesus Christ." When the interviewer inquired about what King would ask Jesus, he said, "I would like to ask Him if He was indeed virgin-born. The answer to that question would define history for me."[3] And define history the virgin birth does. Not only does Jesus's miraculous conception point to His divinity but it also made a way for God to save His people. If Christ were not born of a virgin and instead had Joseph as His natural father, He could not have been the sacrifice, holy and pure, that He needed to be. Because Jesus was born of Mary, within a line of human ancestors stretching back to Adam (Luke 3:23–38), He could represent His brothers and sisters. And because He was born sinless, Jesus could be the perfect sacrifice God required, "without blemish or spot" (1 Peter 1:19).

Both Matthew and Luke attest to the fact that Mary was a virgin, but Matthew cites a prophecy of Isaiah to bolster the claim (1:23). We repeat Isaiah's words along with Matthew each Christmas— "Behold, the virgin shall conceive and bear a son, and shall call his name Immanuel" (Isaiah 7:14)—and we celebrate the miracle of God's plan stretching back into Israel's history, seven hundred years before Christ's birth in Bethlehem. But how much do we really know about Isaiah's prophecy—about the context in which it was uttered and about the controversy surrounding Matthew's use of it?

Long before vile Herod sat on the throne in Jerusalem, another wicked king reigned there. The author of 2 Kings tells us Ahaz "did not do what was right in the eyes of the LORD his God, as his father David had done.... He even burned his son as an offering, according to the despicable practices of the nations whom the LORD drove out before the people of Israel" (16:2–3). And it is to Ahaz that God spoke through Isaiah about the sign of a virgin with child.

Ahaz ruled the southern kingdom of Judah in the shadow of the Assyrian Empire, which threatened to swallow up the known world. The northern kingdom of Israel, along with Aram (also called Syria), her neighbor to the north, trembled at the thought of Assyria's power unleashed. And they looked to Judah's King Ahaz to join with them in an alliance against their common enemy. To put pressure on Ahaz, the two kingdoms invaded the land of Judah, taking men, women, and treasure captive (2 Kings 16:5; 2 Chronicles 28:5–15). The message was simple: you're either for us or you're against us.

It is with these wolves at the door that Isaiah speaks God's words to King Ahaz, imploring him to trust the Lord wholeheartedly. Since God knows Ahaz is a man of little faith, He invites the king to ask Him for a sign—anything at all, "deep as Sheol or high as heaven" (Isaiah 7:11). But trusting God means trusting God alone—no deals, no military allies, and no other gods—and that's a price Ahaz is unwilling to pay. He refuses God's offer of a sign, and he refuses to trust the Lord.

This is when Isaiah utters those famous words: "Therefore the Lord himself will give you a sign. Behold, the virgin shall conceive and bear a son, and shall call his name Immanuel" (7:14). Despite Ahaz's lack of faith, God gives him a sign and promises to deliver the nation of Judah from the threat of Israel and Syria. A sign-child will be born, and while he's still very young, Israel and Syria will be laid waste (see 7:15–17).

History unfolds just as God had declared. Ahaz asks Tiglath-pileser, the king of Assyria, for help defeating Israel and Aram, and since the two nations are already on Tiglath-pileser's list of lands to be conquered for his empire, he obliges. But in exchange, Judah becomes a vassal-state of Assyria, and Ahaz must pay Tiglath-pileser tribute year after year for the privilege (2 Kings 16:7–9). Judah may be safe temporarily, but the price of her security, and for Ahaz's lack of faith in God, is steep. Tiglath-pileser, vassal-states, and wicked King Ahaz seem about a million miles away from Christmas, but it was in this foreign world of imperial threats and cowardly kings that God first spoke of the virgin birth.

The original child born of a "virgin" was Isaiah's own son (see Isaiah 8:3–4). But the Hebrew word that's translated "virgin" in Isaiah 7:14 can also simply mean, "young woman." There is no indication of anything miraculous in the conception of this boy. Isaiah and his wife seem to have gone about things the old-fashioned way. And his being called "God with us" does not imply that the boy would be anything more than human. Rather, this description is intended to show how God would deal with His people—He wouldn't abandon them (see Hosea 1:2–11 for other examples of this kind of message-name being given to children).

Matthew is sometimes accused of borrowing from Isaiah's prophecy without warrant. The charge is sometimes leveled that the boy born to a "young woman" in Isaiah has nothing to do with a virgin birth or the coming of Christ at all. And it even appears, according to Isaiah himself, that the prophecy saw its fulfillment in the lifetime of King Ahaz. But I believe that God did have Jesus in mind as He spoke to the wicked man who occupied His Son's future throne, so I believe that Matthew got things right after all.

While it is true that the Hebrew word *'almâ* means "young woman" and is not the technical term for "virgin," it is strange that the more typical word for "woman" or "wife" is not used here in Isaiah 7. The chosen term, though not restricted to virgins, is used for any woman of marrying age—a woman who is to remain a virgin until the day her marriage is consummated. And this idea of implied virginity is so connected to the Hebrew term that when Jewish scribes, centuries later, sat down to translate Isaiah into Greek, they used the word *parthenos*, which carries the most basic and common meaning, "virgin." It appears God had chosen the words He placed upon Isaiah's lips very carefully, not going so far that they couldn't apply to the present situation but leaving the door wide open for a future, more miraculous fulfillment too.

There's something else peculiar about this prophecy—another instance where God's choice of words makes all the difference. Isaiah says it is the young woman, the child's mother, who will call him Immanuel. Traditionally, it is the father of a Jewish child who provides the name. We see this, for example, in the story of John the Baptist's birth. The whole house looks to Zechariah to see what the boy will be called (Luke 1:62–63). And in the original context of Isaiah's prophecy, the father of the boy is present and available to name him. In fact, the father of the child—Isaiah—is speaking the very words of the prophecy! Yet God insists that it is the woman who will call him Immanuel. Could it be that God is looking forward to another fulfillment of this prophecy, to a time when a young virgin will give birth to a child who has no earthly father to name Him? When Matthew quotes Isaiah's prophecy, he says, "*They* shall call him Immanuel" (Matthew 1:23; emphasis added), perhaps citing a variant text or allowing for Joseph's inclusion in the story.[4] But the peculiarity in Isaiah's prophecy remains, and it speaks volumes about our God who writes history—even as He reveals His plans through His prophets ahead of time.

When we step back from Isaiah's words to take in a larger view of the world in which they were given, and when we consider the king to whom they were delivered, we can see a beautiful picture of the gospel. Ahaz was a man who rejected God and His ways. So disinterested was he in the things of the Lord that he even passed up an opportunity to receive a miraculous sign from Him. But God promises to be with the people of Judah all the same. God extends grace and sends rescue to a nation in rebellion so some people might recognize that grace, turn to Him, and be saved. Seven hundred years later, God will extend grace and send rescue to a rebellious people once again. "[Jesus] came to his own, and his own people did not receive him. But to all who did receive him, who believed in his name, he gave the right to become children of God" (John 1:11–12). At the heart of the gospel is Immanuel—"God with us"—who steps into history to rescue a people often too proud and too stubborn to even know they need rescuing. But He steps into history all the same.

18

A Son Is Given

GENESIS 12:1–3; 15:1–6; ISAIAH 9:1–7

For to us a child is born, to us a son is given; and the government shall be upon his shoulder, and his name shall be called Wonderful Counselor, Mighty God, Everlasting Father, Prince of Peace. Of the increase of his government and of peace there will be no end.

—Isaiah 9:6–7

You'll get two Christmases," a friend told me after I confided in him that my parents were getting a divorce. But to my young heart, it didn't feel like I was gaining anything at all; it always felt like losing. Every year on Christmas Eve, my dad would pick up my sister, my brother, and me and drive us across town to his house for a big Christmas Eve meal and a long night of opening presents. One set of cousins, an aunt and uncle, and my grandmother were sometimes there, but usually, the house was filled with "steps"— step-cousins, step-aunts and step-uncles, step-grandparents, and other "steps" who were connected to us in one way or another through my stepmother, though I wasn't always quite sure how.

I'm sure my dad meant well, filling the house with lots of people and presents, and pulling out all the stops to celebrate Christmas one day early, but what I wanted most for Christmas during those years, whether I could have verbalized it or not, was a normal family holiday with my mom and dad at home on Christmas morning. When divorce shatters a family though, *normal* gets shattered too.

As the years went by and the Norman Rockwell Christmas I longed for didn't materialize, the Christmas season became a time of joy mixed with disappointment, a celebration of hope saddled by the weight of loss. I could empathize with the many people who think of the holiday season mostly as a thing to endure. Our stories may be unique, and each of us may be nursing a different longing, but not one of us has found the Merry Christmas we're looking for—at least not one that lasts.

Disappointment is, of course, not confined to the Christmas season. About two thousand years before Christ, there lived a man who knew the ache of loss all too well. His name was Abram, and his family was broken like mine, though not exactly like mine; his was broken before it could even get started. Abram's wife, Sarai, was barren and beyond childbearing age, so the couple had no sons or daughters. The name *Abram* means "exalted father," so every time Abram's name was spoken, he had a pointed reminder that he would probably never know the joys of fatherhood. That was until one day, when God called him and promised to bless him, not with one son or daughter, but with sons and daughters more numerous than the stars in the sky (Genesis 12:2; 15:2–6).

If Abram's story were a made-for-TV Christmas movie, this promise would give way to a tidy yet magical happy-ending moment. Abram would return to his tent to find Sarai knitting blue booties, caressing a baby bump, and beaming from ear to ear. The couple would embrace and share a silhouetted kiss against the breaking dawn. There might even be some magical Middle Eastern snow. It's a Christmas miracle!

But that isn't how their story goes. Abram and Sarai (later renamed Abraham and Sarah by the Lord) wait twenty-five years for the birth of their son, Isaac, the first star in the sky to be counted.

Those twenty-five years are filled with mistakes and scars and battles and longing—even a misguided attempt to produce the child of promise through another woman. Then once Isaac finally arrives and is growing into the young man Abraham had always dreamed he would be, God tells Abraham to do the unthinkable: put his son to death. Not exactly the stuff of Merry Christmas Hallmark endings.

Abraham climbs a mountain in Moriah with Isaac in tow, preparing to take the life of his only son. It's a scene too shocking and cruel for our modern sensibilities. How could God command a child sacrifice? Why would God want Abraham to give back the gift for which he had waited so long? In the end, God stays Abraham's hand, provides an animal sacrifice, and Isaac is saved. Abraham has passed the test. He has been tried and proven faithful. For Abraham, God is more satisfying, more wonderful, than any gift he has received—including his only son. There isn't anything for which he would trade his friendship with God. And even though he can't always understand God, he trusts Him implicitly (Genesis 22:8).

This kind of trust is what God desires from all His people. But trust like Abraham's is wild and untamed, and as the nation God promised to Abraham grows up, the people often find it easier to trust in chariots and earthly powers—even false gods. About 1,300 years after Abraham first met God, there is a king on Judah's throne who is nothing like Abraham—he neither values nor trusts God. He is King Ahaz, and under his leadership, the nation is mired in sin. Although Ahaz has already refused to listen to God, God continues to speak. A time of judgment is coming, the prophet Isaiah tells him. But amid warnings of a coming invasion and future destruction, Isaiah looks ahead to another child of promise: "For to us a child is born, to us a son is given; and the government shall be upon his shoulder, and his name shall be called Wonderful Counselor, Mighty God, Everlasting Father, Prince of Peace" (Isaiah 9:6).

Peace. That's what I really wanted for Christmas all those years ago. The loss I felt when my parents divorced was a loss of peace.

And it wasn't just because broken homes are prone to more conflict. The Hebrew word for *peace*, used here in Isaiah 9, is *shalom*, and it means much more than its English counterpart. *Shalom* is about wholeness, contentment, rest for the soul, and prosperity in its truest sense. It's what Abraham discovered while walking with the Lord, waiting twenty-five years for Him to deliver on His promise, and it's what gave him the confidence to place his only boy on an altar to be slaughtered. True *shalom* comes from God alone; we can't have it without Him. So God gave the world the Prince of Peace, His only Son, for Christmas.

And God's gift is not just for a few. God gave Jesus to the whole world. Isaiah tells us, "Of the increase of his government and of peace there will be no end" (Isaiah 9:7). Christ's kingdom will last forever and cover the entire earth. One day, every person and every nation will be blessed by His reign. And though Isaiah makes this promise explicit, it's one Abraham would have recognized. God had told him, way back in Genesis 12, "In you, all the families of the earth shall be blessed" (v. 3). It is through Jesus, one of the stars Abraham had counted in that night sky so many years earlier, that God would bless every family and every nation. When Jesus puts on flesh and steps into our world, Abraham can't help but rejoice (John 8:56).

For any of us to truly know God's peace, the chains of sin must be broken, and freedom must be purchased. Like Abraham, God led His Son up a mountain, but for our sake, God did not stay His own hand. For the love of the world, He sacrificed Jesus so we might have *shalom*. Jesus paid the price for our sin and made a way for us to enter into His ever-expanding, never-ending kingdom of peace. The hope of Christmas can't be found in a Hallmark Channel moment or in some perfect set of circumstances. It can only be found in Jesus Christ, the one Christmas present that never disappoints.

19

The Faith to Be a Pregnant Virgin

LUKE 1:26–38

And Mary said, "Behold, I am the servant of the Lord; let it be to me according to your word."

—Luke 1:38

These days, Christmas at our house can be intense. With three young boys, December has more energy in it than Tigger hopped up on espresso. It's easy to forget how different things were when Laurin and I celebrated our first son's very first Christmas.

Back then, things were a bit more peaceful. Jonah was just a few months old, and we were still getting used to this little person living in our house and pulling our heartstrings. In those early days of his life, he seemed to change and grow every day. And with each newfound skill and baby breakthrough he made, Laurin and I beamed with pride. Jonah's world was relatively small back then. We didn't really know what he would like and what he wouldn't, which activities would set his heart on fire and which would leave him cold. We just didn't know: Would he have a good sense of humor and laugh a lot? Would he love the outdoors? Or computers?

What kind of music would he like? Would he enjoy reading? Or playing sports? Or cooking?

God knit Jonah together in His own image and according to His good plan, so I have no doubt he'll continue to be amazing just the way he is. It's been fun for Laurin and me to discover, right along with Jonah, just how God has wired him. And more surprises and growth are in store. I wondered back then—and I wonder now—what kind of father I will be as he grows. I ask myself if I have what it takes to be the man Jonah needs me to be, and I pray that my son will see a heart in me that reflects God's.

When Jonah arrived, I became a prepper. Not unlike people who stockpile dried food and water in preparation for the zombie apocalypse or a hurricane, I found myself wanting to be prepared for anything and everything that life throws my way. For Laurin, prepping began several months before Jonah was born. Her nesting instincts kicked in at full strength shortly after we found out she was pregnant. While Jonah was still in utero, our home received upgrades and a makeover, we bought baby products that I didn't even know existed a short time earlier, and we filled a closet to the ceiling with diapers and wipes—enough so that, barring an attempt at a Guinness record for diaper changing, we would never again need to buy diapers for the little guy. (Yes, we still had some left when our second son was born.)

Jonah's birth pushed Laurin and me into the deep end of the parenting pool, so we counted on the Lord, on each other, and on the sage advice of those who had gone down this path before us to keep us from drowning. It's been a humbling journey—I never realized how much I didn't know about having a baby or being a parent. Now when I read about Mary and her visit from Gabriel, I have a whole new appreciation and respect for the teenage virgin and her willingness to be used by God.

Mary has two responses to the news that she will be the mother of God's Son. First, she asks, "How will this be, since I am a virgin?" (Luke 1:34). Unlike Zechariah, who also questioned news of a miraculous birth from Gabriel, Mary does not ask out of disbelief but out of innocent, wide-eyed wonder. Second, she lays aside her own plans and ambitions: "Behold, I am the servant of the Lord; let it be to me according to your word" (1:38). But it's not what she says to Gabriel that I find most remarkable; it's what she doesn't say. She doesn't ask, "What about Joseph? What will he think?" She doesn't try to explain to the angel the social stigma that may attach itself to her as a pregnant and merely betrothed Jewish girl. She seems to have no concern for her own safety or provision—only for God's will.

Had Joseph gone through with his plan to divorce Mary quietly (Matthew 1:19), Mary most likely would have been labeled an adulteress and could have remained an object of scandal for the rest of her life. As it turns out, Joseph was a noble man and obedient to the Lord, so Mary, it seems, was saved from the shame and gossip that would have surrounded her otherwise. But as Gabriel stands before her, Mary does not know how Joseph will respond to the news that she is pregnant by the Holy Spirit. She must have assumed her story would sound pretty crazy to her betrothed—and to everyone else as well.

Mary's response to the angel, then, embodies the kind of life that her Son Jesus would later call His disciples to live:

> Do not be anxious, saying, "What shall we eat?" or "What shall we drink?" or "What shall we wear?" For the Gentiles seek after all these things, and your heavenly Father knows that you need them all. But seek first the kingdom of God and his righteousness, and all these things will be added to you." (Matthew 6:31–33)

Mary's trust is not in Joseph's goodness (although he proved to be very good), nor is it in the kindness of the Nazarene people. Instead, she trusts in God—in the power of His coming kingdom and in His lavish provision.

With a heart and an attitude like Mary's, it's easy to forget that she was likely only fourteen or fifteen years old when she received her angelic visitor. No one would have expected that all of God's dealings with Israel were leading to this. As C. S. Lewis noted, "The whole thing narrows and narrows, until at last it comes down to a little point, small as the point of a spear—a Jewish girl at her prayers."[5] The Bible doesn't tell us anything about Mary's parents—Jesus's grandparents—but I have to believe they were pretty amazing people to raise the kind of daughter they did. When I think about the fourteen- or fifteen-year-olds I know, or about myself at that age, Mary's response to Gabriel's news is even more astounding. That's because from our earliest days on earth as small children, the message we receive from this world is that we must take care of ourselves. It's one of those truths that is both good and twisted at the same time.

We parents want our kids to be self-sufficient, responsible, and respectful of others. The Bible is replete with commandments that require people to care for their own needs, as well as the needs of others. God tells parents, "Train up a child in the way he should go" (Proverbs 22:6). Presumably, that training includes preparing him to be a productive member of society who works to meet his own needs and the needs of his family as long as he is able. And in the New Testament, Paul tells the Christians in Thessalonica, "If anyone is not willing to work, let him not eat" (2 Thessalonians 3:10).

But there is a moment when responsibility can turn into idolatry. When we fail to remember that everything we have—even those things gained through our own hard work—comes from God, we no longer depend on Him for our daily bread. Instead, like Adam and Eve before us, we begin to chart our own course and set ourselves up as the gods of our own universes, as if we are the final answer to our every desire and our every need.

The gospel and God's kingdom appear upside down in comparison. Jesus said, "For whoever would save his life will lose it, but whoever loses his life for my sake will save it" (Luke 9:24).

The world tells us we ought to do everything we can to preserve our own lives—and so does Jesus, but Jesus knows that true life can only be found in God's kingdom. So He tells His followers to hold on to this life loosely, looking instead to the Father and His kingdom.

Mary personifies this teaching of Jesus. Her eyes are fixed on God, and she willingly follows Him, though the place He is leading may be uncomfortable and dangerous. As I said, without knowing a thing about them, I think Mary's parents must have been wonderful people to raise such a daughter. As Laurin and I look forward to many more Christmas celebrations with Jonah and his brothers, my prayer is that we will become the same kind of people. I pray that each of our boys, like Mary, will be responsible with all that God entrusts to him and wildly obedient to the plans of his heavenly Father, no matter where they might lead him. And not just the kids, Lord. Me too.

20

The Long-Awaited Day

LUKE 2:22–38

And there was a prophetess, Anna, the daughter of Phanuel, of the tribe of Asher. She was advanced in years, having lived with her husband seven years from when she was a virgin, and then as a widow until she was eighty-four.

—Luke 2:36–37

For more than ninety years, Rockefeller Center in Manhattan has been the display case for one of the world's most famous and beautifully adorned Christmas trees. Each year, a multistate search is undertaken to find the perfect evergreen—one that tops all the others. The chosen tree must be at least sixty-five feet high and forty-five feet wide, and it cannot be more than one hundred ten feet high. (If it's any larger, it will be too big to navigate the streets of New York City.) The largest tree on record was set up in 1999 and measured one hundred feet, two inches high. On average, the tree weighs more than ten tons, and it's adorned with over forty thousand LED lights and a nine-foot-wide Swarovski crystal star.

Having grown up in the Connecticut suburbs of New York City, I've seen the tree in front of 30 Rockefeller Plaza dozens of times.

It really is beautiful; the image on a television screen doesn't quite do it justice. So, as I stood two hundred miles to the north one Christmas many years ago, looking up at another tree—this one in Boston Common—I was not all that impressed. It was a big tree—somewhere in the neighborhood of forty to fifty feet high—and it was decorated with thousands of sparkling lights, but it just wasn't the sight that New York's tree usually is.

The tree set up in Boston every year, however, is no ordinary tree. It's an annual gift from the people of Nova Scotia, Canada. On December 6, 1917, two ships collided in Halifax Harbour, causing an explosion that wiped out nearly half of the city. Two thousand people were killed, and thousands more were injured in the devastation. The people of Boston, after learning of the emergency by telegraph, mobilized help and responded. A crippling blizzard blocked the way, but the people of Boston pushed through. The doctors, nurses, and medical supplies that arrived by train were the first major help the people of Halifax received following the explosion. So, each year the people of Nova Scotia give a Christmas gift to the people of Boston—a large evergreen to adorn the city at Christmastime.

Knowing the story behind the tree in Boston, I prefer it to the tree in New York. Boston's tree is a reminder of the best qualities people can muster, including a willingness to help those in need—strangers-turned-neighbors by the kind of sacrificial love Jesus described in the parable of the good Samaritan (Luke 10:25–37). It may not be as big, have as many lights, or get the same attention as the Rockefeller Center tree, but to me, the tree in Boston Common is much more beautiful. Appearance is not the only measure of a thing.

On the outside, Simeon and Anna must not have seemed like much. When we bump into them in Luke's gospel on the day of Jesus's presentation at the temple, they're both very old. Simeon is so old that he recognizes the only thing keeping him alive is a promise from God. We read, "And it had been revealed to him by the Holy Spirit that he would not see death before he had seen the Lord's Christ" (2:26). Anna too is described as "advanced in years" (2:36). She had been married, but for only seven years before her husband died. On the next detail, the text of the original Greek is a bit unclear: She's either eighty-four years old when we meet her here in the temple complex or she's lived as a widow for eighty-four years, which would make her about one hundred five years old in this scene. Either way, she has seen a lot of life.

Today it's common to discount the elderly. Our society worships youth—we want to be young, stay young, and pretend we're young, no matter how old we get. But God doesn't seem to hold the same view. Simeon and Anna have been tested and tried by life, and they have remained faithful. They also exhibit tremendous patience and trust in the Lord, waiting not just months and years, but generations, to see God act to rescue His people. That kind of character—that kind of relationship with God—cannot be cultivated overnight. Their devotion didn't earn them the right to greet Jesus, but it did prepare them.

At different moments that day, Simeon and Anna each see the baby Jesus and recognize Him as the Messiah. But I think it's more appropriate to say that God recognized them. There was nothing particularly remarkable about Jesus's appearance. To any onlooker, He was just a baby—probably one of several being dedicated at the temple that day. But two senior citizens see more than just a baby; they see the hope of Israel and the world. Simeon and Anna are given eyes to see the truth in much the same way that others, years later, would see more than a carpenter or a traveling miracle worker. Jesus's identity would be revealed to them by their heavenly Father (see Matthew 16:15–17).

What makes Simeon and Anna compelling, then, is not some list of qualifications they hold or some Sherlock Holmes–like attention to detail that allows them to see what no one else can. Rather, what is most beautiful about Simeon and Anna is the power of God in their lives.

On the outside, that tree in Boston simply doesn't compare with its New York City counterpart. And the same could be said for Simeon or Anna, if you were to see either of them praying in the temple alongside a priest or Levite. By worldly standards, Simeon and Anna are people forgotten and overlooked, an old man and an old woman long past their prime. Anna, being from the tribe of Asher (Luke 2:36), should be considered especially forgotten, since Asher was a tribe thought to be completely lost after the people of northern Israel were taken captive by the Assyrians centuries earlier. But God chooses her, along with Simeon, some filthy shepherds, and a few wise foreigners, to be among the first to welcome His Son into this world.

Think about the irony of the situation: Jesus, the Messiah that the nation has been waiting for, is brought into the temple, the center of religious life in Israel. And the Jewish leaders—the priests and the Levites, the scribes and the elders—don't recognize Him. These men, who are supposed to be walking in close step with the Lord and who were charged with leading God's people, miss Him entirely. Instead, two out-of-touch and out-of-date prayer-warriors receive Him and celebrate His arrival.

Simeon and Anna's old age puts them in a previous generation, so in a sense, they are a symbol of Israel's past. But I think we should also see them as a clue to Israel's future—and our present. Anna is called a prophetess (Luke 2:36), and we read that Simeon came to the temple "in the Spirit" and spoke prophetic words to Mary and Joseph (Luke 2:27–35). They both experienced the power of the Holy Spirit in their lives before Pentecost (Acts 2). That was a rare thing in the Old Testament period, reserved for people God had called to a special task. But one of the amazing promises for the New Testament era is that God gives His Spirit to all who come to know Jesus as Lord and Savior.

It's a theme that shows up over and over again in the Bible. God chooses a young man with a slingshot to take down a giant (1 Samuel 17). He delivers the city of Samaria using four broken-down lepers (2 Kings 7:3–15). And forty days after the first Christmas, He reveals His one and only Son to a couple of old-timers in the temple. Today, most incredibly, He chooses to work through "jars of clay" (2 Corinthians 4:7)—people like you and me in whom He has graciously placed His Spirit. Apparently, appearance is not the only measure of a thing in God's eyes either.

21

A Christmas Message
from Heaven

DANIEL 9; LUKE 1:8–17, 26–38

And the angel answered him, "I am Gabriel. I stand in the presence of God, and I was sent to speak to you and to bring you this good news."

—Luke 1:19

On the top of our Christmas tree each year is an angel. It's basically a plastic cone with arms, wings, and a haloed head—glossed to look as if one of the heavenly host is wearing a shiny, white ball gown. When it comes time to put her on the tree (and I'm pretty sure it's a *her*), I'm always afraid I'll break her. The years have made her quite delicate. I'm not quite sure how old the angel is, but judging by the style and colors, I think she's from the 1960s. She isn't much to look at, but our angel will probably be a part of our Christmas traditions for the long haul—for as many years as I can manage to get her to the top of our tree without accidentally breaking her. I'm always careful with our angel because she's special to Laurin. The angel belonged to her mother, who passed away just a few years ago.

I love knowing that our angel has sat at the top of other Christmas trees and presided over other Christmases, and that her painted-on, plastic eyes have seen many gifts unwrapped, plenty of hugs given, and lots of joy bestowed. And who knows—it just might be that someday our children or grandchildren will take up the angel and invite her to oversee their Christmas celebrations. Even though she's fragile and poorly made, she may continue on long after Laurin and I have gone on to glory.

Angels are like that. They get to see generations come and go, and they get to watch as God's plans move from promise to fulfillment—even if hundreds or thousands of years separate the two. Of course, I don't mean plastic tree-topper angels. I'm talking about the angels of God who serve Him in the heavenly realms and as His messengers here on earth. Unlike the human actors in God's grand story of redemption, who only get to see God's work in their own corner of the world and who can only play their parts for a short time, the angels have been watching since the beginning. And at various times and at God's direction, they have stepped through the veil separating heaven and earth to be included in the story.

Most times, the angels in Scripture go unnamed. It seems that who they are is less important than what God has sent them to do or say. But there are a couple of exceptions to their usual anonymity, and Gabriel is one of them. We first encounter the angel Gabriel in the book of Daniel. There, he helps to unravel mysteries surrounding world events as they relate to God's people and His plans in history. Later, Gabriel shows up in Luke's gospel—more than five hundred years in the future from Daniel's perspective—to share good news with Zechariah and with Mary.

In each case, when Gabriel arrives on the scene, his very appearance strikes fear into the hearts of those he visits (Daniel 8:17; Luke 1:13, 30). He is neither cute nor fragile like the angel atop our tree or the myriad angels depicted on ornaments and

Christmas cards. But he does not come to bring judgment either. Instead, with each visit, he offers a message from the Lord about how history is about to bend to bring about the kind of goodness that reflects its Creator.

Gabriel visits Daniel twice (see Daniel 8–9). The first time it's to provide an interpretation of a vision Daniel has seen concerning the nations of the world and the destiny of God's people. Gabriel's second visit is in response to Daniel's prayers. An eighty-year-old Daniel confesses his sins and the sins of Israel, and Gabriel arrives with news of how God will deal with sin, once and for all: "Seventy weeks are decreed about your people and your holy city [Jerusalem], to finish the transgression, to put an end to sin, and to atone for iniquity, to bring in everlasting righteousness" (9:24). While there is a great deal of debate over how we should understand these seventy "weeks," most Bible scholars recognize that Gabriel is lifting Daniel's eyes to see the coming of Jesus. So it's fitting that when the "fullness of time" comes (Galatians 4:4), Gabriel is the one to make the birth announcements for both John the Baptist and Jesus.

Gabriel moves when heaven moves, but God could act without letting His people know His plans or His timetable. John the Baptist would have still been John the Baptist had Elizabeth miraculously conceived without a word from an angelic ambassador. And Jesus would have still been born the Son of God without Mary and Joseph being in on the plot. Circumstances would most certainly have been different, but God is not bound by circumstances and could have brought His redemption to bear without giving a preview to any of us here on earth. God sending His messenger Gabriel, then, is an act of love. Just as a parent softly prepares a child when life is about to change, God, through His servant Gabriel, gently tells Zechariah and Mary how their lives are about to take a turn, about how their stories are about to be forever entwined with the story of His Son.

God's grace resounds in the words Gabriel offers to Zechariah and to Mary. Just as he told Daniel, "You are greatly loved" (Daniel

9:23), he tells Zechariah, "Your prayer has been heard" (Luke 1:13), and Mary, "You have found favor with God" (Luke 1:30). In these statements of reassurance, Gabriel discloses the Father's good heart toward His children. And for those who can receive it, this is the message God brings to us today, the same words of blessing Gabriel brought to Daniel, Zechariah, and Mary: *You are loved, I hear your prayers, and My favor is with you.* Every moment of Jesus's life, every excruciating moment of Jesus's death, and every ounce of resurrection glory shout loudly that these things are so. This is God's message for the world at Christmas, if only we will hear it.

22

Ghosts of Christmas Past

MATTHEW 2:13–15

And he rose and took the child and his mother by night and departed to Egypt.

—Matthew 2:14

There is nothing Ebenezer Scrooge can do to change the things he has done. As the Ghost of Christmas Past shuffles Scrooge from one memory to the next, dread is the only response he can muster as the painful scenes pass before him. Confronted with the truth that he has spent the time he has been given as a despicable, selfish man, he knows he deserves nothing but contempt and isolation in this life, and eternal torment in the next. Perhaps the worst part for Scrooge is having to relive his memories in real-life detail while being powerless to step in and change the past, being unable to speak to his younger self and set things right.

By the end of the story, the redemptive power of a repentant heart wins out, and the pain that Scrooge experiences while walking through his past regrets is overcome by the joy of generosity and love—the Christmas spirit lived out. Every year, the familiar story of *A Christmas Carol* by Charles Dickens is retold with cartoon animals, Muppets, and famous British actors. No matter how long we live, seeing redemption on display never gets old. But like every tale of good conquering evil and sin succumbing to love, there are scars of time that cannot be erased. Regardless of what Scrooge does with the time he has left in this world, nothing he can do will make up for the time he has lost. Broken promises, past regrets, and wasted Christmases cannot be relived. The Ghost of Christmas Past, therefore, seems the cruelest of all.

Even in the grand story of redemption—the one that fills the pages of the Bible and kindles hope in hearts that have been born again—there is a large question mark hanging over the past. In one sense, we know how the story will end. The book of Revelation tells us, "And he who was seated on the throne said, 'Behold, I am making all things new'" (21:5). I believe that when God says that *all things* will be made new, He means it. Somehow and in some way, even our mistakes and broken promises from long ago will be made new. We don't know how this will be, but through a miracle we cannot yet understand, every tear will be wiped away in God's presence (Revelation 21:4), including our tears of regret.

The nation of Israel was a nation of regret. Although she had been rescued out of slavery by the hand of God and made His chosen people among all the nations, Israel had failed to keep her promises. As a wife to her husband, she had been unfaithful time and time again, giving herself to the powers of this world and to the dark gods of her neighbors. And Israel had reaped what she had sown. She saw her kingdom divided and splintered, and she was taken away into exile. But God was faithful to her. Despite her persistent disobedience, He graciously brought His people back into the promised land. As the New Testament opens, the Jewish people have nothing to stand upon—nothing except their own regrets and God's grace.

The covenant that God made with Israel had always been one of conditions—blessings for obedience and curses for disobedience (see Deuteronomy 28–29). From the exodus onward, Israel's history had been a record of her disobedience. There were a few bright moments to celebrate—people like Boaz, David, and Elijah—but even these are stained with sin. Sin can be forgiven, but what's done is done. So like Ebenezer Scrooge's journey through Christmases past, the Old Testament is an unchanging record of regrets and mistakes. If only there were a way to live through that history again, for Israel to do things differently the second time around.

At Christmas, Jesus came to earth to secure a blessed future for all those who would follow Him. He did this by dying on Calvary, paying the wages of sin that we had all earned. But He also came to relive the past for the nation of Israel. Jesus came to be the Israel that Israel could never be—perfectly obedient and perfectly fulfilling God's law. In doing so, He was able to give His people the blameless record that, right from the start, they had marred.

Matthew tells us that shortly after the wise men visit Jesus, Mary, and Joseph, an angel appears to Joseph in a dream and warns him of Herod's murderous designs, saying, "Rise, take the child and his mother, and flee to Egypt, and remain there until I tell you" (2:13). Joseph does as the angel instructs, though I wonder what went through his mind as he led his family on their ninety-mile journey under cover of darkness. It must have seemed strange to Joseph. After all, the baby in his care was the Son of God. Surely, heaven's warriors would protect Him from any harm that might come His way. Why, then, was a trip to Egypt necessary?

Just as Caesar's census had brought Joseph and Mary to Bethlehem, the rage of Herod sent the holy family to Egypt. And once again, the machinations of a king were nothing more than tools God used to bring His plans to bear. "This was to fulfill what the Lord had spoken by the prophet, 'Out of Egypt I called my son,'" explains Matthew (2:15; compare Hosea 11:1). Some scholars argue that Matthew hijacked this verse from the book of Hosea, retroactively making it a prophecy about Jesus that neither Hosea nor God intended. A straightforward reading of the original passage in Hosea shows it was not originally a prediction about the

Messiah but a statement about the history of Israel. Still, I don't think Matthew is misusing the verse; I think he understands it perfectly. By spending time in Egypt, Jesus is fulfilling—in a sense, He's reliving—what God's people, Israel, had already experienced.

And it doesn't stop there. Jesus passes through the waters of baptism (3:13–17), just as the Israelites passed through the waters of the Red Sea. Then the Spirit leads Him out into the desert for forty days of testing (4:1–11), just as the Hebrew people were led by God into the desert for forty years of testing. These parallels are more than mere coincidence. Jesus is taking on the identity of Israel, living out the nation's history. And by becoming Israel, Jesus does what His fellow Israelites never could. He lives up to Israel's end of the covenant—perfectly obeying every law and statute, leaning on His Father in holy dependence—so that all of God's blessings could belong to His people. This was a miracle few expected.

At Christmas, God put on skin to obey the law He knew His people could not. And then, on Good Friday, He paid the price for sin He knew they could not pay. By becoming one of His people, the Son made a way for the children of Israel to become like Him: children of God. Now, anyone who trusts in Christ— Jew and Gentile alike—can become a true Israelite and receive the blessings Jesus earned. Because of Jesus's perfect life, credited to all those who know Him as Lord and Savior, we need not fear our past mistakes. Jesus has given us a past without regret.

23

Light from the Fire

JOHN 14:15–31; 16:5–16

"And I will ask the Father, and he will give you another Helper, to be with you forever."

—John 14:16

He fills Zechariah and Elizabeth, and their son John before he is even born (Luke 1:15, 41, 67). He comes upon Mary in power, overshadowing her the way He had once hovered over the primordial sea (1:35; compare Genesis 1:2). He moves in Simeon's life, revealing the hidden things of God and enabling him to prophesy (Luke 2:25–32). And then there's Anna, who's called a prophetess (2:36); He discloses Jesus's true identity to her too.

Have you figured out who *He* is?

Although we don't often think about the Holy Spirit when we consider the Christmas story, the Spirit shows up on just about every page. And while the outpouring of God's Spirit in power is some thirty-three-plus years removed from Jesus's birth—described not in the Gospels, but in Acts 2—the stage for Pentecost was set at Christmas.

Luke, the author of Luke and Acts, does not see a great divide between the work Jesus began in His earthly ministry (recorded in the gospel of Luke) and the work He continues to do through His disciples (the beginning of which is recorded in the book of Acts; see 1:1–2). We ought not be surprised, then, to see the Spirit at work in the story of Jesus's birth. After all, Christmas is all about God coming near—and that's precisely what the Holy Spirit does.

The angel Gabriel tells Mary, "The Holy Spirit will come upon you, and the power of the Most High will overshadow you" (Luke 1:35). In a mysterious way that Scripture does not detail further, it is the Holy Spirit who causes Mary to conceive. She, of course, is a virgin—and will remain a virgin until after she gives birth to Jesus (Matthew 1:25)—so the miracle of Jesus's conception is nothing short of impossible. Or at least it would be if the Holy Spirit were not involved. As Gabriel reports, "Nothing will be impossible with God" (Luke 1:37).

The Holy Spirit is in the business of breathing life into places where life cannot grow. He does it with Mary the virgin and with barren Elizabeth. But He also brings life through Zechariah (Luke 1:67–79) and later through Simeon and Anna at the temple (Luke 2:25–38), as their prophetic words offer hope to Israel and to the world. These Christmas encounters with the Holy Spirit are a preview of the new life that will be available in the kingdom Jesus is bringing.

The Bible is clear that apart from Christ, we are dead in our sins (Ephesians 2:1), and it is the Spirit who brings life out of death (John 6:63). It is the life-giving Spirit who testifies about Jesus (John 15:26), who convicts the world of sin (John 16:8), and who opens eyes to the truth (John 16:13), changing hearts and minds. And that same Spirit who raised Jesus from the dead now lives within every follower of Christ (Romans 8:11).

He seals us (Ephesians 1:13), leads us (Romans 8:14), reminds us of the truth (John 14:26), helps us (John 14:16), empowers us (Acts 1:8), and speaks to us (Acts 11:12; 13:2). He produces the fruit of "love, joy, peace, patience, kindness, goodness, faithfulness, gentleness, [and] self-control" in our lives (Galatians 5:22–23). And He gives every believer gifts—each of which is an expression and display of God himself, building up and bringing life to the body of Christ (1 Corinthians 12:7).

The Holy Spirit has always been at work. We see Him clearly in the lives of men and women throughout the Old Testament. But those experiences of the Spirit were limited to certain individuals— often prophets, priests, kings, judges, and folks like that—and His influence was often temporary, sometimes only lasting for a short season while there was a task to be done or a role to play in salvation history.

But with Jesus's death and resurrection, a new age has dawned. The Holy Spirit, God himself, now lives inside His people. As Peter says, echoing the prophet Joel:

> And in the last days it shall be, God declares, that I will pour out my Spirit on all flesh, and your sons and your daughters shall prophesy, and your young men shall see visions, and your old men shall dream dreams; even on my male servants and female servants in those days I will pour out my Spirit, and they shall prophesy. (Acts 2:17–18; compare Joel 2:28–32)

With the coming of the Holy Spirit, everything has changed. We are now free to live in constant communion with God because He is always with us, guiding our steps and making us more like Jesus as we surrender to Him. We are living in a reality that the Old Testament saints could only have hoped for (Numbers 11:29; Ezekiel 36:26–27). Back then, only the high priest got to come close to the manifest presence of God—in the temple's Most Holy Place, and just once a year on the Day of Atonement (Leviticus 16; Hebrews 9:7). But after Jesus made a once-and-for-all sacrifice for sin—the very sacrifice that all the Old Testament sacrifices pointed toward—the curtain that barred entrance to the Most Holy Place was torn in two (Matthew 27:51; Mark 15:38). Because of Jesus's shed blood, we have access to God, and He has access to us. God's Spirit is now closer to us than our own skin. This is why, at the end of His earthly life, Jesus could say to His disciples, "Nevertheless, I tell you the truth: it is to your advantage that I go away, for if I do not go away, the Helper will not come to you. But if I go, I will send him to you" (John 16:7).

God used dreams, angelic messengers, and even the stars in the sky to prepare the way that first Christmas, but it was the Holy Spirit who breathed life into men and women as God got ready to do something rather impossible—send His Son into the world. It's easy to read the Christmas story and think that the men and women God used were somehow unique, altogether different from you and me. But they were ordinary, sinful, broken people. What made them special was God's Spirit—the same Spirit who dwells inside all those who know Christ today.

The incarnation was, of course, a special event, and one that won't ever be repeated. But the Holy Spirit still breathes life where there is none. He still speaks, and He still heals. And God is still at work in this world, bringing the kingdom of light to places where there is only darkness. He uses people like Mary and Zechariah, Simeon and Anna—people just like you and me, who have been quickened by the Spirit of God.

24

The Mom Who Saved Christmas

LUKE 2:16–20

But Mary treasured up all these things, pondering them in her heart.

—Luke 2:19

When I was a kid, I had a Lionel electric train set. My dad bought it for me for Christmas one year, though I was so young I don't remember ever not having it. It was my favorite thing about decorating for Christmas. While everyone else in my family was fussing with lights, delicately arranging ornaments, and setting up stockings, I was laying out the tracks for my train set around our Christmas tree. Once it was all connected and plugged in, the black locomotive and its four cars would make their way around the tree, chugging along like magic.

Although I only pulled it out at Christmastime, over the years the train took some damage from my brother and me. A few of the plastic cars broke, and a handful of pieces went missing. And when I became a teenager, I stopped setting it up for Christmas altogether. It no longer claimed the same place in my imagination it once did. So for years the train sat in its original box, which was held together by packing tape, in our basement.

When I was in my late twenties and living far from home, my mom called and asked if I still wanted that old train set. She and my stepfather were getting ready to move, and she had run into a man who collected antique toy trains and was willing to buy it. At that point in my life, I didn't really have room to store it, and I remembered that it had missing pieces and broken cars; I told my mother to go ahead and sell it. But now, as my wife and I are trying to put down roots and create our own Christmas traditions, I find myself longing for that electric train set, wanting to pass it down to my sons, Jonah, Jude, and Luke. Though I don't remember what that toy collector paid me for my train, it wasn't nearly enough.

When we experience joy, we want to hold on to it, not only to remember and to relive that joy, but also to pass it on to others. Our joy increases when it's shared. After the shepherds found Jesus in the manger, they shared their story—about the glory that shone, and the angels, and what those heavenly messengers said about Jesus. Luke tells us, "Mary treasured up all these things, pondering them in her heart" (2:19). And it's a good thing she did.

Have you ever thought about what happened to the cast of characters who were there that first Christmas? Joseph appears to have died before Jesus's public ministry began. The shepherds and wise men dispersed shortly after worshipping their newborn King. Zechariah, Elizabeth, Simeon, and Anna were all very old to begin with; they surely went home to be with the Lord during Jesus's childhood. By the time Jesus had suffered and died and been raised to new life, the only one left to tell the tale of Christmas was Mary. So when it came time for Christ's followers to take pen to papyrus and record the events of His life, it was Mary who shared about Jesus's birth and the miraculous events that surrounded it. Without Mary's memories, there would be no record of the first Christmas and no way for us to look back and celebrate.

Mary's joy spread to Jesus's early followers, and they in turn shared that joy with people all over the ancient world. Those folks continued to spread the joy of Christmas year after year and generation after generation. Everywhere the gospel broke new ground, the story of Christmas went with it. And now it is our turn.

At Christmastime, the world turns red and green. Lights are hung, stars and angels are put on display, and "White Christmas" is in the air. Though it may seem that Jesus's birth has been pushed back into a corner in favor of Santa Claus and Black Friday sales, there is a cultural memory of joy everywhere you go during the holiday season. Even those who have never darkened the doorway of a church somehow know that Christmas is supposed to be a time of peace, love, and hope. We who know the King in the manger have a tremendous opportunity to tell people what Christmas is all about, to offer up a reason for the joy our friends, neighbors, and coworkers are longing to find. We may lament the commercialization of Christmas, but every activity of the season provides us with a cultural bridge on which to share Jesus.

Like Mary all those years ago, we can share our joy, not merely because the story of Christmas is true, but because we have partaken of its truth. While no one living on earth today can claim to have been an actual eyewitness to the events of the first Christmas, we can still be witnesses for Christ. Every authentic follower of Jesus has met the Savior and knows Him personally. In fact, the Spirit of God has taken up residence within the hearts of His people. We can now speak of Jesus's birth—as well as His life, death, resurrection, and glorious reign—as men and women who have experienced His presence firsthand. The most powerful evidence for the truth of the gospel lies neither in archaeology nor in historical evidence for the resurrection. The most compelling arguments for its truth are our own stories of life change and the ongoing work of the Holy Spirit in our lives.

There's an electric train out there gathering dust in someone's collection. My guess is that it's sitting lifeless, never again to take a turn around its tracks. But it's a great toy; I know from personal experience. A few Christmases back, I bought Jonah a toy train just like it. Every year, we pull that train out of the attic, and I watch as Jonah and his brothers take turns sending that little locomotive round and round our tree. They play for hours at a time, filling the gondola car with Legos and Lincoln Logs while making the most amazing train sounds. Still, I don't think they enjoy that train nearly as much as I enjoy watching them play with it. Joy is best when it's shared with others.

25

Three Boxes for Christmas

JOHN 17:1–26

And they went with haste and found Mary and Joseph, and the baby lying in a manger.

—Luke 2:16

I know of parents who, in an attempt to stave off greed and materialism in the hearts of their children, limit the number of Christmas presents each child receives to three. Why three? The thinking goes like this: If three gifts—gold, frankincense, and myrrh—were enough for Jesus, then three wrapped packages under the tree should be enough for any child.

There is a part of me that loves the thought of keeping Christmas simple, of making sure it's about more than the gifts. But there is also a part of me that sees Christmas as a time to be extravagant with the people we love because our heavenly Father was extravagant with His love for the world on the night Jesus was born. Christmas should always be about more than getting gifts, but it should also certainly be a day unlike any other—a day to love one another with reckless abandon. Then again, it may be that having three boxes under the tree will serve as the greatest reminder of God's amazing grace after all—because, as it turns out, the story of redemption, wrapped up at Christmas, is the story of three boxes too.

The manger is one of these boxes. Though we tend to think of the Christmas manger as a wooden stand filled with hay, feeding troughs in the ancient Near East were typically made of stone. The trough that exists in our imaginations comes from Renaissance art, where a typical Western European manger was often pictured. The makeshift crib where Mary placed the baby Jesus was likely a hollowed out, rectangular block of stone—a simple container designed to last a lifetime and withstand the abuses of hungry animals coming to feed. In the incarnation, we have the most extraordinary of miracles: the infinite God of the universe placed inside such a box.

But the manger is really the second box to cradle the presence of God. In the Old Testament, God had instructed the Israelites to build another box. This one—the ark of the covenant—arrived early for the first Christmas by about 1,500 years. It was a wooden chest wrapped in gold, and it was the place where God's presence dwelt among His people, the place where heaven and earth met.

Of course, God cannot really be contained in any box. He is everywhere. As David writes,

> Where shall I go from your Spirit? Or where shall I flee from your presence? If I ascend to heaven, you are there! If I make my bed in Sheol, you are there! If I take the wings of the morning and dwell in the uttermost parts of the sea, even there your hand shall lead me, and your right hand shall hold me. (Psalm 139:7–10)

But in a special and mysterious way—a way that even the world's greatest theologians cannot quite wrap their heads around—God allowed His presence to be with the ark. He did this so His people would have a visible, tangible reminder of His love for them and of His holiness.

The ark was a symbol of the covenant God had made with His people—a covenant of law and sacrifice, of blessings and curses; it was a covenant based on God's perfection. Since God is utterly holy—thoroughly good, true, and beautiful—nothing sinful can enter into His presence without being destroyed. The law God gave to Israel contained prescriptions for dealing with sin and brokenness, sacrifices that would cover over sins and ritual impurities so that corrupt and wicked people might continue to walk with Him. But the ark was like the God it represented: holy. No ordinary Israelite could come near—and certainly no one could touch it. The ark was always to remain at a distance, representing the distance between God and His people that had been imposed by sin.

Only through blood could one man, the high priest, approach the first box—the ark—and then, only one day a year. But the second box—the manger—invites all to draw near. Luke records that the shepherds on that first Christmas night "went with haste and found Mary and Joseph, and the baby lying in a manger" (2:16). No one in the Old Testament would have dreamed of approaching the ark in such a hurry. Just compare the shepherds' experience with that of Uzzah, one of the men who helped transport the ark to Jerusalem under King David:

> And when they came to the threshing floor of Nacon, Uzzah put out his hand to the ark of God and took hold of it, for the oxen stumbled. And the anger of the LORD was kindled against Uzzah, and God struck him down there because of his error, and he died there beside the ark of God. (2 Samuel 6:6–7; compare 1 Chronicles 13:9–10)

By all accounts, Uzzah's intentions were good; he was trying to keep the ark from falling off its cart and smashing to the ground. And he still died. But that's the point: No matter how good our intentions are, because of sin, we will never be able to draw near to God's holiness. That's what the manger—the second box—is all about. We can't come to Him, so He comes to us. Jesus left His heavenly home to come to earth. Wrapped in flesh, He laid aside His glory so He could be close to the people He created. All are welcome to gather around the manger-crib—filthy shepherds straight from the fields, Gentile astronomers bearing lavish gifts, those who are looking for the Messiah, and those who are not. There is no danger of an Uzzah-event happening at the manger; our invitation is borne out of God's grace and not our own righteousness.

But God is not content with merely joining us in our broken world; He wants us to live with Him forever. And that's why there's a third box in this grand story.

In Jesus's day, the people of Israel had a unique burial tradition. When someone died, his or her body would be placed in an above-ground tomb, wrapped up in strips of linen but laid out on a bench. Over the course of the following year, the person's body would decompose, and on the anniversary of the death, the family of the deceased would return to the tomb for a "second burial." The bones would be collected and placed in a small limestone box called an ossuary. The ossuary would then be placed on a shelf inside the tomb alongside the bone-boxes of family members who had previously died.

After Jesus breathed His last and was taken down from the cross, Joseph of Arimathea and Nicodemus (both secret disciples of the Lord) retrieved His body and placed it in an aboveground tomb—wrapping it in cloth strips and preparing it with burial spices (John 19:38–42). But no one returned a year later for the "second burial" part of the tradition. That's because Jesus didn't stay dead. His sacrifice on the cross was payment for our sins, and God raised His Son up on that first Easter morning to show the world that the way had been made for us to be with Him forever.

When Jesus died, the Bible tells us, "the curtain of the temple was torn in two, from top to bottom" (Matthew 27:51). This curtain, or veil, guarded the Most Holy Place in the Jewish temple, the room that had once housed the ark of the covenant. The curtain was sixty feet high, thirty feet wide, and about four inches thick; the only one who could tear it in two is God himself. But because He did so, those of us who know Jesus Christ—who have given our lives to Him and have accepted His sacrifice on our behalf—are now free to enter into God's holy presence. Nothing can ever separate us from His love, not even our own sin. Because the third box of Christmas—Jesus's ossuary—never existed, we can rest knowing that we have eternal life, the greatest Christmas present of all.

Jesus said, "This is eternal life, that they know you the only true God, and Jesus Christ whom you have sent" (John 17:3). And that's what Christmas is all about: God creating a way, through the life, death, and resurrection of His Son, Jesus, for us to have eternal life. We can spend our time on earth walking closely with Him and all the days afterward in His eternal embrace. We were created to know the goodness, truth, and beauty that come from the hand of the Father. At Christmas we celebrate the moment when Goodness, Truth, and Beauty himself was born of a virgin and placed in a manger.

As we've already seen, God cannot be contained within a box. If we look around, we can see rays of His goodness peeking through the clouds, glimmers of His truth sparkling in the rain, and echoes of His beauty drowning out the noise that surrounds us. There will come a time when the earth will be overtaken; heaven will come down, and God's glory will cover every square inch of this world. On that glorious day, we will, perhaps, pause for a moment while being overwhelmed with wonder to remember that this whole thing started with the first outpost of His goodness—a manger in the small town of Bethlehem.

Putting Together the Birth Narratives to Find the Christmas Story

Many years ago, when I was a sophomore in college, my friend Jeb and I were driving back to school from a semester break when we got caught in a terrible snowstorm on the Massachusetts Turnpike. Very quickly the roads turned treacherous, and the visibility grew poor. By the time the weather got really bad, we were too far from home to turn back and afraid that if we stopped, we might get stuck. In the moment, it made more sense for us to continue on our trip, even if we were moving at a snail's pace.

Before long, I could see the limits of the road only by the guardrails on either side of the highway, and I was doing my best to keep my car's tires in the tracks left by the eighteen-wheeler in front of us. Eventually, though, the weather won. My small Volkswagen slid and spun and went off the road in one of the few places for miles without guardrails. Actually, we made our unplanned stop in a small ditch just in front of a rest stop—the only one for an hour in either direction, given our limited traveling speed. We had to wait until the next morning for a tow truck to help us get back on our way, but Jeb and I were both thankful to be out of the storm, safe and warm.

I share this story to illustrate the grace of God-given guardrails. They can help us stay on the road, not only by providing us with visual markers as guides, but also by giving us a gentle nudge if we begin to skid into danger. Without them, we might end up stranded on the side of the road and waiting for a tow truck. The nativity narratives in Matthew and Luke are like guardrails for careful Bible reading. Though the two evangelists share their own thoughtful accounts of Jesus's birth, the Holy Spirit inspired both men. Therefore, it just won't do to give preferential treatment to one version of the story over the other, as if to say, for example, that Luke got the details right but Matthew was mistaken. Both men got the story right—so their accounts should fit together without sacrificing bits of one or the other.

It seems that Matthew and Luke wrote independently of one another, but a harmony of their unique Christmas stories is still possible—and even necessary. For if one section of Scripture cannot be reconciled with any other, we must concede that the Bible is like that house divided against itself: unable to stand (Mark 3:25). The Holy Spirit, as the divine Author, made no mistake when guiding the minds and pens of His evangelists. We can be confident that even in places where it may seem nearly impossible to put our two stories together, our puzzle has a solution.

What follows is merely one person's attempt at putting the pieces together; it is certainly not the only way to understand the story of Jesus's birth. But my hope is that, as we walk together through the first Christmas, leaning on the shoulders of both Matthew and Luke, we will gain a deeper appreciation for both narratives—and more importantly, a greater joy in knowing more of what God has accomplished through the birth of His Son.

Mary's Pregnancy and Joseph's Faithfulness

Luke tells us about the birth of John the Baptist, a subject on which Matthew is silent, so Luke 1:5–25 stands on its own without need of reconciliation. However, when we move into the foretelling of Jesus's birth, Matthew fills out the story with information we can't find in Luke, namely Joseph's angel-dreams and his obedience to the Lord.

Reading about Joseph's experience helps us make sense of Mary's. In particular, it's commonly believed that Mary, the unwed mother-to-be, faced scorn and shame from her own family and neighbors in Nazareth when her pregnancy was discovered. But Matthew tells us Joseph "resolved to divorce her quietly" (1:19). In other words, no one save the angel Gabriel, Mary, and Joseph knew that she was expecting; otherwise, the divorce could hardly have taken place quietly.

Since Luke doesn't include Joseph's plan to divorce Mary or the visitation of an angel in Joseph's dreams, we can't be sure whether Mary told Joseph about her pregnancy and then went to stay with her cousin Elizabeth or if she shared the big news once she came back. It seems more likely that Mary broke the news to Joseph after she returned from her trip, since Luke tells us Mary "went with haste" to see Elizabeth in Judah.

Coming back home to Nazareth at about three months along (Luke 1:56), Mary would have successfully avoided her family and neighbors during the worst of her morning sickness, but her body may have begun to show signs of pregnancy. Joseph's decision concerning divorce would have needed to be made quickly, and that is the sense we gain from Matthew, who tells us that Joseph "did as the angel of the Lord commanded him" when he "woke from sleep" (1:24).

Once Joseph resolved to believe God's messenger—and his beloved—the couple began living together as husband and wife, though they did not consummate their marriage until after Jesus was born.[6] Any rumors circulating about Mary's supposed impropriety would have lost traction. Even though Mary's baby bump may have begun to show just as she started her married life with Joseph, there's little reason to believe it would have given her early pregnancy away. Mary would not have worn the types of tight-fitting clothes we wear today, and at the end of her first trimester, there would be little to notice anyway. Besides, once

Joseph took Mary into his home as his wife, there would be no need to keep the secret. She could be pregnant (though, publicly, not quite as far along) without fear of humiliation.

There's another reason to believe that Mary's pregnancy was never considered scandalous. If the gossips in Nazareth had thought that Jesus was conceived in sin, such a rumor would have been prime ammunition for Jesus's enemies to use during His preaching and healing ministry. Jesus's opposition brought up other details from His background to "prove" He wasn't a prophet, let alone the Messiah (see John 7:52), yet we don't hear an allegation of illegitimate birth leveled against Jesus. The closest we get to such an insinuation is in Mark's gospel, when Jesus is preaching in the synagogue at Nazareth. Those gathered there are astonished at his teaching and say, "Is not this the carpenter, *the son of Mary* and brother of James and Joses and Judas and Simon? And are not his sisters here with us?" (6:3; emphasis added). But the people who ask these questions are not Pharisees or scribes or priests—the ones who would plot against Jesus years later. These are just regular folks, members of the community who had known Jesus most of His life. Most likely, they refer to Him as "the son of Mary," rather than of Joseph, because Joseph had already passed away.[7]

These nativity accounts in Matthew and Luke are not primarily about Joseph and Mary, though both of their lives provide us with beautiful examples of unfettered submission to the Lord. Joseph, it appears, never bore the public embarrassment of marrying a young woman everyone thought unfaithful, and Mary was not considered the town harlot, suffering shame for a sin she didn't commit. Instead, God provided for the couple and made a way through a seemingly impossible situation. After all, it would be Jesus who would marry a truly unfaithful bride—the church—and it would be Jesus who would suffer for sins He never committed. Those burdens were His to bear, and all the glory for doing so belongs to Him alone.

The Journey to Bethlehem and Jesus's Birth

Only Luke tells us about the Roman census that brought Joseph and Mary to Bethlehem, but he doesn't tell us precisely when, on Mary's pregnancy timetable, the trip took place. All he says is that "while they were there, the time came for her to give birth" (2:6). It's often assumed that registering for the census would take only a few days, so it must have been that Mary was full-term when Joseph got the call to go to Bethlehem and that Mary came along because of the very real possibility she could give birth at any moment. Alternatively, it's been supposed that Mary went with Joseph because the people of Nazareth had turned against her when they discovered she was pregnant. But neither of these scenarios seem likely.

If Mary were about to have her baby, traveling would be a strange thing to do. It would make more sense, even if Joseph had been called out of town, for Mary to stay at home, surrounded by her family, perhaps being helped by her own mother. As we've already seen, it doesn't appear that Mary ever faced public shame over her pregnancy. If Mary went to Bethlehem with Joseph because her parents and her neighbors ostracized her so severely, then, again, why didn't such a scandal (not a small thing in conservative Jewish circles of the first century) follow Jesus into His ministry?

I'd like to suggest that it was by choice that Mary went with Joseph to Bethlehem, that the couple may have been there for some time before Jesus was born, and that they may have even planned to stay in Bethlehem for good. I realize these suggestions may sound absurd given the Christmas plays we've all seen, but I think it makes the best sense of the details included in the two gospels.

Concerning Jesus, the angel Gabriel told Mary, "He will be great and will be called the Son of the Most High. And the Lord God will give to him the throne of his father David, and he will reign over the house of Jacob forever, and of his kingdom there will be no end" (Luke 1:32–33). Similarly, the angel who appeared to Joseph in a dream said, "That which is conceived in her is from the

Holy Spirit. She will bear a son, and you shall call his name Jesus, for he will save his people from their sins" (Matthew 1:20–21). Mary and Joseph knew that Jesus would be the Messiah—and as faithful Jews, they would have known the Messiah was supposed to come from Bethlehem, David's hometown. I imagine there was a smile across Joseph's face when he was ordered to Bethlehem for the census. *So that's how God is going to get us to Bethlehem so the baby can be born there*, he must have thought.

The prophecy linking the Messiah to Bethlehem says, "But you, O Bethlehem Ephrathah, who are too little to be among the clans of Judah, from you shall come forth for me one who is to be ruler in Israel, whose coming forth is from of old, from ancient days" (Micah 5:2). It seems that Mary and Joseph saw this verse not only as an indication of the coming King's birthplace but also of His hometown. So Mary and Joseph may have planned to relocate to Bethlehem for good—to raise Jesus there, in the same place where their ancestor David had grown up.

The family, of course, does return to Nazareth, and Jesus grows up there in Galilee. But there is a mention of other intentions in Matthew's gospel. Sometime after Jesus is born in Bethlehem, an angel warns Joseph of Herod's intention to kill the child and instructs him to escape to Egypt with Mary and Jesus. When Herod dies, the angel once again appears to Joseph and tells him it's safe to return to Israel, so they make arrangements to head back. "But when [Joseph] heard that Archelaus was reigning over Judea in place of his father Herod, he was afraid to go there, and being warned in a dream he withdrew to the district of Galilee" (2:22). Did you catch that? Joseph and Mary had planned to go back to Bethlehem in Judea—not to Nazareth—when they returned home from Egypt. It seems their original trip to the City of David for the census was supposed to have been a permanent move.

Mary and Joseph's arrival in Bethlehem is often portrayed as frantic, rather than as part of a plan. The scene usually plays out like this: They reach town late at night, only to search unsuccessfully for a comfortable place to stay; there's "no place for them in the inn" (Luke 2:7). But at last the couple finds someone willing to let them hunker down in a stable, or perhaps a cave, so that Mary, now well into her labor, can give birth to the Son of God and place Him in a manger.

But if the couple was planning on staying in Bethlehem for the duration, it only seems right that they would have made better travel arrangements. And even if moving to Bethlehem for good was only an afterthought dreamed up by Joseph while in Egypt, nowhere does the Bible suggest that Mary went into labor the night she and Joseph arrived in Bethlehem. Again, Luke simply tells us "while they were there, the time came for her to give birth" (2:6). They may have arrived a day, a week—or even several months—before it was time for Mary to have her baby. There's simply no reason to believe that Mary and Joseph were in a panic or that God's provision for the couple was meager in any way. I'm sure there were a few surprises for Mary and Joseph the night Jesus was born but something more in line with what other expectant parents go through.

Some will object that since the couple tries to find lodging at an inn, they must have just arrived in Bethlehem as Mary started to feel contractions—and the use of a manger for a makeshift cradle shows that Jesus was born in a stable or a cave, surrounded by animals. But the word that has been traditionally translated "inn" in Luke's gospel is probably better understood as "guest room." It's the same word used later in Luke to describe the upper room where Jesus and His disciples share a Passover meal on the night He was arrested and tried (22:11).[8]

Mary and Joseph were not hoping to make last-minute hotel reservations. Rather, they were likely staying in the home of some of Joseph's relatives—after all, his family was from Bethlehem. But because so many people were in town for the census and the guest room was otherwise occupied, Mary was given the lower room in the small house in which to labor. It would have been the place where animals bedded down on cold nights, though there is no mention of animals being housed there that night. It would also have been the most comfortable and private room in an otherwise crowded house. Such a room was a common feature for houses in Israel during the first century. This version of events may also be supported by Matthew's gospel, which tells us the family was staying in a "house" in Bethlehem (2:11).[9]

The night Jesus entered this world, God provided abundantly—in ways we may not have previously realized. Despite being far from home in a strange, new city, Mary had a place to stay, a husband to care for her, and a healthy birth. When God calls us, He equips us. But the greatest way He rescued Mary that night was not by giving her a roof over her head or safety during childbirth. God gave Mary that which we all desperately need: a Savior. That first Christmas night He was given to all who would receive Him, but Mary alone was afforded the honor of laying His head down to rest inside a straw-filled manger.

The Shepherds and the Wise Men

The gospel accounts keep the shepherds and the wise men far apart—just like a classic crèche with herdsmen on one side of the manger and magi on the other. The wise men follow a star in the east and travel to Bethlehem to find the King of the Jews, but they make an appearance only in Matthew. Angels burst through the nighttime sky to tell shepherds in the fields about the birth of the Messiah, but their scene plays out only in Luke. The two groups of unexpected worshippers never meet.

The shepherds, according to Luke, seek out Jesus on the night He was born (2:11, 15). The wise men, unlike their counterparts in our nativity scenes, don't arrive until sometime later. It's been suggested that they came to Bethlehem some two years after Jesus was born. This may be the case, as it fits the timeline the wise men gave to Herod concerning the star that appeared in the sky; they said it showed up two years prior to their coming (Matthew 2:16). And as we've already seen, it seems Mary and Joseph had planned to settle in Bethlehem following the birth of Jesus (Matthew 2:22). If the wise men really did arrive when the Lord was a toddler, then we should not be surprised to find the family still living in Judea.

But what are we to do with Luke, who seems to have Joseph, Mary, and Jesus leaving the region much sooner? He tells us, "And when they had performed everything according to the Law of the Lord, they returned to Galilee, to their own town of Nazareth" (2:39). This statement comes immediately following Jesus's dedication in the temple—when He's only a few weeks old.

Because an isolated reading of Luke makes it appear that Joseph, Mary, and Jesus were only very short-term residents of Bethlehem, some have argued that maybe our nativity scenes aren't too far off after all—that the wise men must have shown up when Jesus was still a newborn. But this can't be the case. When Joseph and Mary bring Jesus to the temple, they offer the sacrifice for Mary's purification prescribed for the poor—"a pair of turtledoves, or two young pigeons" (2:24; compare Leviticus 12:8). For those who could afford to do so, the law commanded a lamb to be sacrificed, but Mary and Joseph could opt only for the birds. This means that when Jesus was forty days old—the number of days required for Mary's purification (see Leviticus 12:2–4)—the magi had not yet come. We know this because if these men had arrived, bearing gifts of gold, frankincense, and myrrh, Mary and Joseph would have no longer qualified to give the offering of the poor. They would have had the money to purchase and sacrifice a lamb.

Luke doesn't mention Herod's massacre of babies or the holy family's sojourn in Egypt. His narrative simply jumps from the temple scene where Jesus is dedicated and words of prophecy are spoken over Him to the family's return to Nazareth. That Luke leaves out such a large chunk of the story can be problematic for readers today, but we must remember that Matthew and Luke wrote with different purposes in mind and to distinct audiences.

In this particular instance, we should note that Luke addresses his gospel to a man he calls "most excellent Theophilus" and writes expressly for the purpose that he "may have certainty concerning the things [he had] been taught" (1:3–4). His Greek name is a clue that Theophilus is a Gentile or a Greek-speaking Jew, and the descriptor "most excellent" implies that he is a high-ranking official of some sort. Perhaps he is a recent convert to Christianity but someone with the means to support Luke in the writing of his gospel narrative. It makes sense, then, that Luke would leave out Herod's murder of innocent children in his Christmas account, since he wants to stress that Christ's coming kingdom is a good thing for the world. Though we may not always be able to determine why certain episodes are included in one nativity account and not in the other, we'll want to remember that the Gospels are not modern biographies. Neither Matthew nor Luke wrote with the intention of capturing every consequential detail of Jesus's life.

While the gospel writers are selective in the material they present, they do not distort the basic facts. So if Matthew says the star that the wise men followed had been lighting up the sky for a full two years, we should be in no hurry to usher Joseph, Mary, and Jesus back to Nazareth anytime sooner. Both gospel writers are correct: The family returned to Galilee after fulfilling all the requirements of the law (Luke) but also after a time in Egypt to escape Herod's sword (Matthew). The manger scenes we set out on our tables at Christmastime may not be historically accurate—the shepherds and wise men never gathered together around Jesus—but that isn't really the point anyway. Jesus is King at every moment in time, and those who can recognize Him as such bow down in worship.

Our Father's timing is always perfect, and so are His plans. Though it appears Mary and Joseph headed to Bethlehem with thoughts of making a new life there, God knew their sojourn would be short-lived—at least in Judea. So to prepare the young family for an extended trip to Egypt, He sent wise men from the east with gifts—valuable gifts that would become their means of support for the journey. And when God called them home to Israel, He brought the family back to Nazareth—to friends, family, and neighbors they had given up years earlier. If there had ever been a suspicion about Mary's early pregnancy, there would be none now; enough time had passed, and Jesus had become a small boy. When the Son came to earth, the world was turned upside down for Mary and Joseph, but God was there to put things right side up.

The Lord has given us two narratives of His Son's birth. One on its own would be a great gift, but giving two indicates abundant love. Each is worthy of a mountain of books dedicated to plumbing the depths of God's amazing grace. But when we bring the two stories together, the treasures they contain are multiplied.

As I sat down to write this short appendix, I wondered if perhaps I shouldn't. I love the traditional manger scene—the stable, the star, the wise men, and the shepherds. And I can recall wonderful Christmas sermons about the sacrifices of Mary and Joseph—how they bore undue scorn in order to obey the Lord. The last thing in the world I want to do is to chip away at those cherished traditions—to tear down the stable, so to speak. Rather, my goal has been to show that God's Word is a reliable guide, even when some of the details seem difficult to put together. But mostly, it is my hope that seeing the Bible's wonderfully rich account of the first Christmas in a new light will bring comfort to those who need it most. God is our great provider and a loving Father who can be trusted. Always.

NOTES

1. Sally Lloyd-Jones, *The Jesus Storybook Bible* (Grand Rapids: Zondervan, 2007), 17.

2. See pages 121–122 in the appendix, "A Search for Harmony," for a possible reason as to why Luke chose not to include Herod's murder of the innocents in his gospel account.

3. "The Virgin Birth of Jesus: Fact or Fable?" Religious Tolerance: Ontario Consultants on Religious Tolerance, http://www.religious tolerance.org/virgin_b.htm, quoted in Billy Graham, *The Reason for My Hope* (Nashville: Thomas Nelson, 2013), 78.

4. Note also Luke 1:31, where Gabriel announces to Mary that she will become pregnant: "*You* shall call his name Jesus" (emphasis added). He makes no mention of Joseph in the naming process.

5. C. S. Lewis, "The Grand Miracle" in *God in the Dock: Essays on Theology and Ethics* (Grand Rapids: William B. Eerdmans Publishing Company, 1972), 84.

6. According to Luke 2:5, Mary and Joseph are still "betrothed," rather than married, when they head to Bethlehem. In first-century Israel, betrothal was a much deeper commitment than modern engagement. Once a couple was betrothed, they were, for all intents and purposes, legally married. This is why Joseph was pondering a divorce, not just breaking off the engagement. But Luke notes their status as betrothed because their marriage has not yet been consummated. Even though Joseph has taken Mary into his home, she is still a virgin.

7. Some will point to John 8:41 as a taunt about Jesus's supposed illegitimacy, but the context there specifically concerns the Jews' connection to Abraham, and not Jesus's family line. And since John

makes no mention of the virgin birth in his gospel, it seems unlikely that he intends for his readers to see something there between the lines.

8. Luke uses a different Greek word entirely for the "inn" that shows up in the parable of the good Samaritan, recorded in 10:25–37.

9. Though Matthew does not tell us how old Jesus is when the wise men arrive, the "house" mentioned in Matthew 2:11 may not be, in fact, relevant; the magi's visit seems to have come some two years after Jesus's birth (see 2:16). But even if this is the case, nothing contained in Matthew's gospel contests Jesus being born in a house rather than a stable or cave.

Help us get the word out!

Our Daily Bread Publishing exists to feed the soul
with the Word of God.

If you appreciated this book, please let others know.

- Pick up another copy to give as a gift.
- Share a link to the book or mention it
  on social media.
- Write a review on your blog, on a book-
  seller's website, or at our own site
  (odb.org/store).
- Recommend this book for your church,
  book club, or small group.

Connect with us:

 @ourdailybread

 @ourdailybread

 @ourdailybread

Our Daily Bread Publishing
PO Box 3566
Grand Rapids, Michigan 49501 USA

 books@odb.org